THEORETICAL FRAMEWORKS IN COLLEGE STUDENT RESEARCH

Terrell Lamont Strayhorn

University Press of America,® Inc.
Lanham · Boulder · New York · Toronto · Plymouth, UK

Copyright © 2013 by
University Press of America,® Inc.
4501 Forbes Boulevard
Suite 200
Lanham, Maryland 20706
UPA Acquisitions Department (301) 459-3366

10 Thornbury Road
Plymouth PL6 7PP
United Kingdom

Library of Congress Control Number: 2013930284
ISBN: 978-0-7618-6088-4 (clothbound : alk. paper)
ISBN: 978-0-7618-6089-1 (paperback : alk. paper)
eISBN: 978-0-7618-6090-7

♾™ The paper used in this publication meets the minimum
requirements of American National Standard for Information
Sciences—Permanence of Paper for Printed Library Materials,
ANSI Z39.48-1992

Dedication

This book is dedicated to my parents, Wilber Earl and Linda Faye Strayhorn; my two children, Aliyah Brielle and Tionne Lamont Strayhorn, and my maternal grandmother, Dr. Creola Evelyn Warner, who earned an honorary doctorate for over 50 years of unparalleled professional service as a teacher in the public school systems of North Carolina and Georgia, and perhaps most importantly, who taught me "to love many, trust few," to love to learn, to engage my own curiosity, and to pursue my own dreams even in the face of adverse circumstances. Because of these, I am.

Table of Contents

Foreword

All too often, educational researchers struggle to understand the critical role that theory plays in the development, conduct, and analysis of research on college students. As editor of the *National Association of Student Affairs Professionals* (NASAP) *Journal*, one of the nation's leading refereed journals in the field of higher education and student affairs administration, I have witnessed both the virtues and dangers of using theoretical frameworks while carefully reviewing manuscripts that were submitted to the journal for possible publication. Virtuous treatments tend to identify the framework, define it various elements, and, though rare, explain how the framework influenced the study. On the other hand, there were risks associated with using theoretical frameworks in quantitative and qualitative studies. For instance, at times, authors seemed acutely convinced that the selected framework "fit" their study perfectly, despite rather obvious incongruence, or blithely unaware of the ways in which the selected theory illuminated some aspects of the phenomenon under study while concealing others, as Dr. Strayhorn rightly points out in this volume. A book that not only identifies prevailing theoretical frameworks in higher education, student affairs, and related disciplines, but also explains their constitutive components, illustrates how such theories have been used in college student research, and makes explicit the ways in which theory influences a study is a worthy contribution to our existing literature. And this is exactly what Terrell Strayhorn offers to the field in *Theoretical Frameworks in College Student Research*. In my opinion, as Emeritus Vice President of Student Affairs, Professor of Counselor Education, and Editor of the *NASAP Journal*, I believe this important volume could come at no better time than now when there has been a virtual explosion of research paradigms, research methods, techniques for analysis, and ways of reporting research findings through print and electronic media.

Over my long career, several timeless questions have been raised periodically. What is a theoretical framework? How do you find one? What do you do with it? What if you learn that the framework is less useful than originally assumed? These are all good questions and there are no easy answers. However, Professor Strayhorn attempts to address all of these questions and other dilemmas associated with theory-based studies in *Theoretical Frameworks in College Student Research*. This book is not only an excellent text to be used in higher education graduate classrooms across the nation, but it offers exceptional recommendations for future research, important insights to help unravel the often tangled issues of theoretical versus conceptual frameworks, and countless examples of how a researcher navigates the research process by making a number of implicit and explicit decisions. Strayhorn does an admirable job of demystifying this sequence of conscious and subconscious choices; and, he does so with language that is accessible, descriptive, and, at times, animated.

Theoretical Frameworks in College Student Research makes clear that theory can play a major role in the design, conduct, and analysis of empirical research on college student populations. In a way, it is distinguished from previous volumes on college student theory in the breadth of theories covered, the depth of illustration offered in each chapter, and the inclusion of frameworks from academic disciplines such as sociology, psychology, law, and technology/communications. *Theoretical Frameworks in College Student Research* will likely aid college student educators, policymakers, educational researchers, and students in understanding the role that theory plays in college student research. For this reason, I highly recommend this book to future generations of those in higher education and student affairs.

Melvin Cleveland Terrell, Ph.D.
Vice President of Student Affairs, Emeritus
Professor of Counselor Education

Preface

The idea for this book evolved out of my experiences as a graduate student turned new professor. As a graduate student, I found myself struggling to grasp a complete understanding of what a theoretical framework was, its role in empirical research, and its utility to the research. Now armed with such information, after a few years of studying theoretical frameworks in both quantitative and qualitative research, I find that my own graduate students lack an understanding of and appreciation for the role of theory in conducting research. As a professor of higher education, I tend to work with students who study the impact of college on students. Their confusion over the use and importance of theory in research may be reflective of the fact that the role of theory is rarely disclosed or discussed openly in college impact studies. Still, when it is, it is explicated vaguely or briefly at best.

In fact, during a recent doctoral seminar on research methods, students raised a number of questions about the role of theory in research. Through puzzled looks and uneven, twisted brows, students asked: what is a theoretical framework? How do I find one? How do I use it? What is its purpose? And, one of my favorites, do I *have* to use one? The emphasis placed on "have" seemed to anticipate, even hope for, a transaction in which the professor would exonerate the student from the captivity of theory by simply saying, "No, you don't have to."

Not only did my students raise a myriad of questions about the role of theory in the development and conduct of research, but they demonstrated their limited knowledge about theoretical frameworks. For example, one question on my pre-assessment of the course asked: what is a theoretical framework? Students also were asked to provide a single example. Responses ranged from a theoretical framework is "a reflection of the researcher's stance or belief about knowledge" to "a summary of one's data collection procedures" or even "a simple outline of the paper." Erroneous examples abounded as some students identified case study and even "race" as possible theoretical frameworks. Obvious confusion over the differences between theoretical frameworks and epistemological stances and various methodologies was loud and clear. Equally clear was the fact that my students stood much to gain from the advanced seminar, as did I, being left with more questions than answers about how to teach students about the use of theory in college impact research.

In summer 2005, I set out on an adventure to find tools that would provide guidance for my future students on employing theoretical frameworks in educational research on college students. Much to my dismay, I found only a few expository essays on the topic, very few chapters on even the importance of theory in research, and only one book on how theoretical frameworks shape research studies per se. In fact, I did not *find* the latter source, as it is a recent text edited by two colleagues of mine at the University of Tennessee, Knoxville: Drs. Vincent Anfara and Norma Mertz. Their book, however, discusses the use of 10 theoretical frameworks in qualitative research not college student research or quantitative empirical investigations.

Armed with a review of the literature and an arsenal of anecdotal evidence, I began thinking about writing a book that would address directly this gap in the literature—the use of theory in college student research, particularly college impact studies. My thoughts grew more intense over time and soon after my imagination provided the broad brushstrokes of what would be included in such a text. In late summer, I sent a proposal to University Press of America, Inc. (UPA) and, by fall 2006, I had written drafts of several chapters.

It is my hope that this book will contribute to the body of knowledge in at least one of many ways. First, it might represent a worthy contribution to the national dialogue about theory in educational research. Second, it might be viewed as a powerfully useful tool or guide for undergraduate and graduate students, educational researchers, and faculty members who teach research methods courses. Finally, if nothing else, I hope it begins to address some of the questions posed by my students over the use of theory in research—namely, what is it and how do you use it?

Keep in mind, gentle reader, that these explanations are provided to render the complex, simple; realizing that a degree of accuracy is lost in the process. Indeed, this collection of theories is not exhaustive and was designed to provide a starting place for those who need assistance with understanding the role of theoretical frameworks in college student research.

Future reviewers of this text may wonder why I decided to use my own work as useful illustrations of how theory can be employed in college student research; indeed, countless other examples abound in the extant literature and my work is by no means the exemplar by which other studies should be judged. However, the decision to feature my own work was both important and necessary to the goals of this text as it allowed me to "unpack and unveil" my thinking as I moved through the research process, to share with you on paper what might otherwise go unsaid and unwritten, implied yet rarely admitted, and to make the inexplicit, explicit. With these goals in mind, I release this volume to you.

Terrell L. Strayhorn, Ph.D.
The Ohio State University
Columbus, Ohio

Acknowledgments

Any undertaking of this magnitude leaves the author indebted to a number of individuals.

I want to thank my wonderful research assistants for their help with the articles, upon which this book depends, and the final copyediting of this manuscript. Special thanks to Amanda Blakewood and James DeVita, both former research associates for the Center for Higher Education Research and Policy (CHERP). Members of my research teams at the University of Tennessee, Knoxville (UTK) and The Ohio State University (OSU) also helped to carry out many of the studies that benefited from the use of various theoretical frames. Sincere thanks to DJ Baker, Chrissy Hannon, Karl Jennings, Fred McCall, Ferlin McGaskey, Shanna Pendergrast, Demetrius Richmond, William Roberts-Foster, Eric Stokes, Chutney Walton, and Porche Wynn, all from UTK. Hearty thanks to Fei Bie, Blossom Barrett, Joseph Kitchen, Hyukje Kwon, Leroy Long, Taris Mullins, Todd Suddeth, Derrick Tillman-Kelly, Michael Steven Williams, and Marjorie Dorime-Williams. Without the competent support of my graduate students, this book would not have been possible.

I benefited greatly from the generous financial support of the American College Personnel Association's Commission for Academic Affairs Administrators, the National Association of Student Financial Aid Administrators, the National Science Foundation, the Tennessee Higher Education Commission in partnership with the U.S. Department of Education, and professional development grants available through the Provost's Office at The University of Tennessee, Knoxville.

I've said it before and I must say it again, my family gave me the encouragement and motivation to start this project, especially my son and daughter who enjoy "working with daddy"—Aliyah working tirelessly online to download music from iTunes, Tionne writing a children's book about two dinosaurs (one named Tionne, the other named Terrell), and me working on this book. While my family provided the fuel to start this project, it took the constant support and encouragement of my close friends to sustain me over time, long after I thought I had written the "last line." Special recognition to Jamaal Brown, Ryan Davis, Elias Fishburne, Darren Harris, Melanie Hayden, Leonette Henderson,

Leon Howell, Royel Johnson, Evelyn Leathers, Belinda Bennett McFeeters, Jeremy Morris, Tonya Saddler, and Mario Williams.

I wish to thank several colleagues who study the impact of college on students, the use of theoretical frameworks in research, or a combination of both. Without their contributions to our collective knowledge, my understanding of theoretical frameworks in college student research, while still incomplete, would be far too limited to write an entire book about it. Thus, I recognize the encouragement and support of Grady Bogue, Elizabeth Creamer, Marybeth Gasman, Joan Hirt, Steve Janosik, Adrianna Kezar, Susan Komives, George Kuh, Norma Mertz, Amaury Nora, Robert Palmer, Laura Perna, Jane Redmond, Margaret Sallee, Pat Terenzini, Melvin Terrell, Bill Tierney, and Vincent Tinto. Special recognition to my former advisor, mentor, and lifelong friend, Don Creamer, who inspired me to "play professor." Almost every Wednesday morning during my last year of doctoral study, Don and I met, in his office, to review drafts of my dissertation, argue out differences about measuring student outcomes, and muse about the importance of theory to practice and research. I learned much from my "Wednesdays with Don" and still erupt into laughter when my mind runs back to his timeless adages—"How much theory? Well, how long is a rope?"

Finally, I thank the many graduate students and scholars with whom I spoke and those with whom I worked as I carried out this book project. Our conversations, your questions, and your work served as a basis for my thoughts about the effective use of theory in college student research. Special thanks to Patti Belcher and the editorial staff at UPA. To all of you and those who are implied, but not listed, I offer a multitude of "thanks."

Terrell Lamont Strayhorn, Ph.D.
The Ohio State University

Chapter One

Introduction

Students as well as experienced researchers who employ quantitative methods frequently have trouble identifying and using theoretical frameworks in their research. This trouble is typically centered on finding a theoretical framework that is appropriate for one's purposes and understanding its pervasive effects on the process of conducting college impact research. A number of individuals with whom I spoke while writing this book admitted that they had little command over the theoretical constructs embedded in most developmental theories and could say little about concepts borrowed from psychology, sociology, anthropology, and fields outside of the study of higher education. This is the gap addressed by the present volume—namely, using theory in college impact research.[1]

Using Theory in College Impact Research

Quite often before scholars can mine an idea for its empirical worth, it is necessary to attend to basic definitions and theoretical matters. In this exercise, scholars tend to employ various kinds of conceptual frames (Merriam, 1998); propositions (Argyris & Schon, 1974); abstract categories (LeCompte & Preissle, 1993); conceptual maps (Ausubel, 1963; Strauss, 1995); models (Parker, 1977); stances (Crotty, 1998); frameworks (Anfara & Mertz, 2006; Strayhorn, 2006c); postulations (Astin, 1984); and hypothesized relationships or theories (Lewin, 1936). Theories are useful in that they generally simplify or explain phenomena that might otherwise remain incomprehensibly abstract, unnecessarily complex, or too vague to be operationalized in research on college students. Yet, theory's power is constrained by what Parker (1977) and others call

---

[1] The terms college student research and college impact studies are used interchangeably throughout this volume to refer to empirical research that focuses on college students as the unit of analysis.

one of the paradoxes of theory—any attempt at simplifying the complex gives up a degree of accuracy. Before describing the purpose of this book, I present a brief summary of three sets of theoretical explanations: student development theory, sociocultural theory, and college impact theory.

Student Developmental Theory

Fundamentally, all educators are concerned about student learning and development. Development occurs in different ways at various times across all populations. A set of theories has been posited to facilitate understanding of students' maturation. For instance, psychosocial theory attempts to explain developmental processes such as identity and personality formation. "Another line of plausible explanations often is referred to as cognitive-structural theories. The works of Jean Piaget, William Perry, Lawrence Kohlberg, and Carol Gilligan are highly respected benchmarks for investigating cognitive development over the lifespan" (Strayhorn, 2006c, p. 12).

Student developmental theory is a guide for understanding learning in college. It provides educators with knowledge that can be used to create interventions designed to enhance student learning and growth (Evans, Forney, & Guido-DiBrito, 1998). Thus, developmental theory can be employed to identify factors contributing to the cognitive and affective development of students. The works of several leading theorists are important examples for this discussion: Lawrence Kohlberg, Arthur Chickering, and Jane Loevinger.

Kohlberg (1969) explored the cognitive dimensions of moral reasoning. Building upon the work of Piaget (1977), Kohlberg posited three levels of moral reasoning: pre-conventional, conventional, and post-conventional. He argued that each level of this model represented a qualitatively different orientation toward the self and society. Essentially, the theory describes a shift from an inward, individual perspective towards a more external, universal stance.

Chickering (1969) described seven vectors of development that lead to establishing one's identity: developing competence, managing emotions, moving through autonomy toward interdependence, developing mature interpersonal relationships, establishing identity, developing purpose, and developing integrity. His model focuses principally on identity development during the college years (Chickering & Reisser, 1993). Chickering's model is not rigidly sequential, like most others, and he noted that students tend to move through these vectors at different rates; vectors can interact with one another over time and students often revisit issues associated with vectors they had previously seemed to resolve.

Finally, Loevinger (1976, 1998) explained cognitive growth as ego development. By ego, she refers to that aspect of personality that assigns meaning to experiences. The term ego development refers to hierarchical interrelated patterns of cognitive, interpersonal, and ethical development that create a cohesive epistemology or worldview (Weathersby, 1981). Therefore, each worldview (or stage) represents a qualitatively different way of responding to or making meaning of life experiences. "Loevinger's description of the milestone sequences of ego development consists of: impulsive, self-protective, conformist, conscientious-conformist, conscientious, individualistic, autonomous, and integrated. Each transition from a previous stage to the next represents an individual's restructuring of personality" (Strayhorn, 2006c, p. 38). Final stages are marked by the ability to respect other's autonomy and a heightened respect for individuality, for instance (Loevinger & Wessler, 1970).

A corpus of studies has posited that students make meaning of life experiences and issues of identity in varied and complex ways (e.g., Jones, 1997; Jones & McEwen, 2000; Renn & Bilodeau, 2005; Renn, 2000, 2006, 2007). One example of a cognitive-structural theory that explains the stages through which individuals make meaning of life experiences is Perry's (1968, 1981; 1978) theory. Perry described nine positions that can be grouped into four categories: (1) dualism, (2) multiplicity, (3) relativism, and (4) commitment. Generally, his theory is characterized by a logical progression from simple meanings to more complex modes of reasoning.

Student development theory has been gainfully employed in studies of African American students' problem solving skills in chemistry (Atwater & Alick, 1990); American Indian students' academic persistence (Brown & Robinson Kurpius, 1997); student leaders (e.g., LGBT) of identity-based organizations (Renn, 2006); and even first-year students' adjustment to college (Martin, Swartz-Kulstad, & Madson, 1999). For example, Renn conducted several studies (along with her colleague, Bilodeau) of LGBT student leaders and found evidence "that leaders of LGBT student organizations grew in both sexual orientation identity and leadership identity" (p. 1).

Yet, there are other questions that educational researchers engage. Not only are higher education researchers principally concerned with student development, quite often they want to study students' personal histories or demographic backgrounds and how their capital reservoirs affect short-term and long-term outcomes.

Sociocultural Theory

Increasingly, researchers in higher education employ or augment existing theories with notions borrowed from social, cultural, and human capital theories. For the purposes of this book and in previous work (e.g., Strayhorn, 2008c), I use the term *sociocultural theory* to refer to this entire group of theories (i.e., human, social, and cultural capital) collectively. Not only does this allow me to use one term to refer to three sets of theories, but it also reflects how these understandings are used in postsecondary research. For instance, I borrowed from sociocultural theory to augment a traditional econometric model to study the labor market outcomes of African American college graduates (Strayhorn); I will refer to this study again later in the text.

Generally speaking, human capital theory posits that individuals make investments in education or training to gain additional knowledge, skills, and abilities that are often associated with increased income, higher occupational status, or other monetary benefits. Broadly conceived, human capital refers to the "information, knowledge, skills, and abilities of an individual that can be exchanged in the labor market for returns such as salary, financial rewards, and jobs" (Strayhorn, 2008c, p. 31). It is generally assumed the more education an individual attains, the more human capital one accumulates and thereby the more benefits one can accrue.

Social capital, on the other hand, refers to the information-sharing networks or instrumental, supportive relationships that an individual may have that provide access to information and opportunity (Ceja, 2006). In addition, social capital refers to the social norms, values, and behaviors that affect an individual (Coleman, 1988). Such relationships may lead to advantageous behaviors, opportunities, or outcomes within a social stratum or system (e.g., clubs or groups where membership is open to "rich" only). As Coleman described: "[social capital] makes possible the achievement of certain ends that in its absence would not be possible...and it exists in the relations among people" (p. 98-101). In previous studies, researchers have used social capital theory to understand the role of parents and siblings in the college choice process of Chicana students (Ceja); at-risk youth (Furstenberg & Hughes, 1995); parental support in students' transition to college (Kim & Schneider, 2005); parental involvement and college enrollment among racial/ethnic groups (Perna & Titus, 2005); African American college graduates (Strayhorn, 2008c); and the success of Mexican American students (Ream, 2003; Sanchez, Reyes, & Singh, 2006), to name a few.

Cultural capital is the system of beliefs, tastes, and preferences derived from one's parents or guardians, which typically define an individual's class standing (Bourdieu, 1977a; McDonough, 1997). Understanding cultural capital is important in educational research as a number of scholars have shown that upper-class students inherit, acquire, and develop substantially different forms of cultural capital than working-class youth (Bensimon, 2007; Lareau, 2003; Oakes, Rogers, Lipton, & Morrell, 2002). This is problematic because schools generally reward, acknowledge, and privilege the cultural capital of the dominant classes and systematically devalue that of non-dominant groups (MacLeod, 1995; McCarron & Inkelas, 2006; Villalpando & Solórzano, 2005). Quite often, students activate their social capital (i.e., relationships and networks) to acquire the cultural capital necessary to succeed in college (Pascarella & Terenzini, 1991, 2005). We will return to this point later in the book.

In sum, sociocultural theory allows us to "see" and understand how human, social, and cultural factors operate independently in domains such as education, coalesce and simultaneously influence each other (e.g., quite often student acquire cultural capital from social interactions), and influence important outcomes such as annual earning and job satisfaction. The latter points to a perennial research topic in higher education: how college affects students.

College Impact Theory

A large number of higher education studies are designed to estimate the net effect of college on students (Pascarella & Terenzini, 1991, 2005). In estimating the effects of college programs, services, and experiences on students, a number of conceptual and theoretical frameworks are employed (Astin, 1993; Chickering & Reisser, 1993; Pascarella, 1985; Weidman, 1989). These models underscore that "the impact of college on nearly any student outcome is the result of multiple influences" (Cruce, Wolniak, Seifert, & Pascarella, 2006, p. 367). These influences include pre-college background traits, pre-college experiences, organizational character of one's institution, academic experiences in college, and non-academic or social experiences to name a few.

Traditional college impact theory suggests that college affects students' behaviors, decisions, and educational outcomes, generally speaking. Impact theories tend to concentrate on the origins of change rather than detailed accounts of the processes through which change occurs. Although they are often referred to as theoretical frameworks or "theoretical models," constructions of college's impact on students are less of an attempt to explain the "how and why" of students' development than a conceptual guide to understanding students and their experiences (Pascarella & Terenzini, 2005).

Astin (1991) developed one of the first college impact models which is now commonly referred to as the input-environment-outcome (I-E-O) model. According to this model, student outcomes are functions of two factors including inputs (e.g., demographic traits) and environment (e.g., experiences in college). Several studies have adopted this conceptual frame to examine the effects of background and/or environment influences on student change and growth in college as well as their propensity to behave in certain ways (e.g., Stein, 2007; Strayhorn, 2008b).

Other college impact theories represent modified versions of the model described above. That is, several authors have used expanded frameworks to specify inputs or to identify specific outcomes such as student learning or cognitive development. For instance, Terenzini, Springer, Yaeger, Pascarella, and Nora (1996) posited a version of the college impact model that consists of three phases, moving from students' college expectations through one's transition between high school or work and college to the impact of college on student outcomes such as learning, achievement, or degree attainment. The model is longitudinal in nature and it is built upon the same premise as Astin's original conceptualization.

The model can be further distilled into six constructs: pre-college traits, curricular patterns, in-class experiences, out-of-class experiences, institutional context, and learning outcomes. College experiences, too, can be further understood as both in- and out-of-class experiences. The take home message is simple—the influence of college on any dependent outcome (Y) (e.g., learning, attainment, satisfaction, retention) is multifaceted and complex. College impact theory was developed in an attempt to make the complex, simple realizing that any attempt to render sophistications as simple gives up a degree of accuracy in exchange for simplicity. This goal is related to the book's purpose.

Purpose of this Book

The purpose of this book is to offer those who engage in college student research, especially college impact studies, a framework or tool for understanding the role that theory plays in educational research. Specially, I sought to address the following questions in each chapter that follows: (a) What is theory and what are some theories that can be employed in college student research? (b) What are the central tenets or key concepts of various theories that relate to college students? (c) How has the theory been employed in prior research? (d) How have I used the theory to conduct research on college students? And, (e) How might the theory be used in future research studies?

Intended Audiences

I believe the information presented in this book will be useful to several audiences. First, as mentioned in the preface, I wrote the book with "my mind's eye" on graduate students enrolled in higher education, student affairs administration, college student personnel, sociology, and related degree programs. Students should benefit from the number and type of theories addressed in this book. It may also be helpful to find so many widely used theories under a single cover. This can potentially reduce the amount of time that researchers have to spend in the library hunting for the "lens" that permits them to "see" what might otherwise go unnoticed or completely concealed.

Faculty who teach graduate-level research methods courses might also find material in this volume useful. For example, my faculty colleagues at the University of Tennessee and I often interact with students who face difficulty in either identifying an appropriate theoretical framework on which to ground their study or struggle to understand the meaningful benefits that theory provides. *Theoretical Frameworks in College Student Research* may serve as a useful complement to a textbook on research, assessment, or statistics. Some faculty members may wish to consider using this text in conjunction with Anfara and Mertz's (2006) handbook on theory in qualitative research, especially those who teach theory-based research classes. Faculty members might also find it useful to adopt this book in graduate-level research design courses that require students to engage in independent research (e.g., theses, dissertations). In such instances, it would seem instructive for faculty to review the broad contours and general tenets of the theories presented herein.

Assignments, then, might involve identifying studies in the published literature that employ a single theory and understanding the ways in which different authors use a single theory—how are they similar and different?

There is at least one other group that might benefit from this book, educational researchers. Those who study college students using both qualitative and quantitative methods and analytic techniques stand to gain from the open, frank discussion of theory that characterizes this volume. For instance, two years ago, while attending the annual meeting of the Association for the Study of Higher Education, four doctoral students attending different colleges and universities in the United States approached me. Each of them wanted to set a time to talk with me about their dissertation projects—which ranged from the socialization of graduate students to faculty careers to the institutionalization of academic support programs for Black men in higher education. During each conversation, it became clear that something was missing, something that linked all of the parts that, in isolation, meant nothing but taken together shed light on a meaningful topic or phenomenon. What seemed missing was the theoretical framework. As one student proclaimed, "It's the glue that links all of the individual parts together to explain what you're looking at. It helps you design your study." In fact, it is theory that increases the rigor of empirical research studies, thereby increasing the worth of a study's findings. We'll return to this point in subsequent chapters.

Overview of the Contents

This chapter serves as the introduction to this text and provides a detailed discussion of theoretical frameworks in college student research and a general description of the book's contents. Chapter Two focuses on college student retention theory and how it can be employed in traditional "drop out" studies. Chapter Three briefly describes the evolution of college choice theory and outlines a study that focused on the influence of race, class, and gender on college students' choice. Chapter Four highlights Sanford's (1966) concepts of challenge and support. College impact theory is taken up again in Chapter Five in a national study of first-generation college students. Sense of belonging is the focus of Chapter Six in a study of Latino college students who responded to the *College Student Experiences Questionnaire*. Finally, Chapter Seven recaps the purpose of and key points raised in the book. In addition, a healthy discussion of future research directions may fuel the interests of readers to pursue college student research using theory in new and innovative ways.

Chapter Two

Studying Student Drop Out: Using Theory as a Guiding Framework

"Dropping out of college is a little like the weather: something everyone talks about but no one does anything about" (Astin, 1975, p. 1).

A hallmark of the American system of higher education is reflected in the diversity of its institutional types (Lucas, 1994). According to the 2000 Carnegie classification system, there are approximately 600 liberal arts colleges, 600 comprehensive universities, and nearly 2,000 community colleges in the United States. Research universities are yet another type of institution and there about 260 such campuses in the nation (Carnegie Foundation for the Advancement of Teaching, 2000).

Not only is there diversity in the type of postsecondary institutions, but the system is further enriched by the diversity of its student population. In 2004, approximately 17.3 million students enrolled in postsecondary education (U.S. Department of Education, 2006). Of these, approximately 14.8 million were enrolled at the undergraduate level. This represented about 86 percent of all students; and the majority were women (57 percent). Over time, more and more students from all racial/ethnic groups have enrolled in college. For example, according to the U.S. Department of Education, African Americans increased their representation among higher education students. African Americans represented 9.4 percent of all postsecondary enrollments in 1976 compared to 10.1 percent of all students in 1994. By 2004, this number had increased to 13 percent of all undergraduate students. So, taken together, these trends illustrate that more African American students enroll in college today than 30 years ago (Nettles & Perna, 1997).

Yet, still today, 40-60 percent of all students who enter college leave before earning a bachelor's degree (Astin, 1975; Braxton, 2000c; Tinto, 1993). These numbers can be even higher among historically underrepre-

sented racial minorities, such as African Americans, who face a number of significant challenges in adjusting to the academic and social systems of college (Tinto). Recent data show that Black men complete college at an even lower rate than their female and non-Black counterparts (Cuyjet & Associates, 2006; Roach, 2001). For example, 1.4 million bachelor's degrees were conferred upon students in 2004; only 9 percent were awarded to African Americans. Perhaps even
more dramatic, only 3 percent of these degrees were awarded to Black men. Part of this reflects the increasing gap between the number of Black men who *enter* college and those who "drop out" before completing their degree. Therefore, African American male attrition is a significant problem that warrants serious attention. To examine this issue in depth, I designed a quantitative study to identify the factors that influence attrition using a nationally representative sample.

The Study

To illustrate the use of theory as a guiding framework in studying college student attrition, I refer to my national study of African American men in 4-year institutions under consideration at higher education journals. In this study, I used a weighted sample of 2,410 African American undergraduate men enrolled at approximately 71 four-year institutions to measure the impact of selected factors on their decision to withdraw from college. These individuals entered college in the fall of 1995 and were surveyed in 1995, 1998, and 2001. The second follow-up study elicited information about their degree attainment and provided a means to study attrition decisions.

In short, 57 percent of all African American males in the sample failed to persist in college by 2001. On the other hand, less than 35 percent of Black men earned their degree within five to six years of initially enrolling in college. Significant predictors of attrition, which separate persisters from those who did not persist, included: parent's level of education, high school grade point average, and social integration.

Despite being an African American male who has earned a doctorate and successfully navigated the American system of higher education, particularly predominantly White campus environments, I deliberately began my study without a thesis (Henstrand, 2006). Instead, I studied the literature on college student attrition in search of a theoretical framework that would guide the development of my study. I was predisposed to using Tinto's (1993) interactionalist theory of college student departure, but I scoured the literature to make sure this was the most appropriate frame.

The Theoretical Framework

It is still true that few topics in higher education have received as much attention as student attrition (also studied as persistence). Over the past 30 years, the vast majority of studies cover this issue in a variety of institutional settings (Baker & Pomerantz, 2000-2001; Canady, 2007); for various types of students (Arredondo & Knight, 2005-2006; Austin & McDermott, 2003-2004); and using a number of theoretical perspectives (Baird, 1993; Strayhorn, 2005). For example, researchers have developed and modified theories of college student departure from college that have been shown to help explain the causal processes that lead students to leave their institutions prior to degree completion (Tinto, 1998, p. 167).

In the early 1970s, Spady (1970) put forth a theoretical proposition to describe the process of dropping out of college. He arrived at the conclusion that social integration plays an important role in the decision making process. In his analysis of college attrition, Spady found that social integration, measured by friendship support, intellectual development, academic performance, and shared values was significantly related to persistence. Figure 2.1 outlines Spady's model.

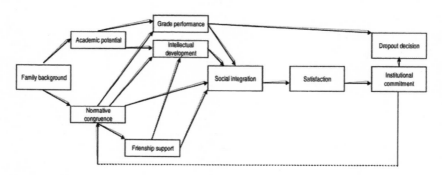

Figure 1. Theoretically Based Model of the Undergraduate Dropout Process

The existing research on college student departure suggests that there are other factors related to whether a student stays in or drops out of school (Bean & Metzner, 1985; Metzner & Bean, 1987). These factors include, but are not limited to, finances, hours of employment, outside encouragement, family responsibilities, satisfaction, stress, and race/ethnicity. In their study, Metzner and Bean (1987) gathered data from 624 nontraditional (commuter, part-time) undergraduates at a midwestern urban university. They found that nontraditional students fail to persist for academic reasons such as low grades and non-academic reasons including lack of the commitment necessary to stay in school.

Still, a large body of persistence research is based on another theoretical model that suggests one must understand a student's integration into the academic and social realms of college to understand his or her decision to stay or leave (Astin, 1975; Bean, 1982; Tinto, 1975, 1987, 1993). Tinto posited that students enter college with pre-college experiences and background traits that influence their educational expectations and commitments. These commitments change during the college years as a result of their integration or "fit" into the academic and social life of the institution. The degree to which students integrate or adjust into these systems is significantly and directly related to their decision to persist. Figure 2. 2 presents a graphical depiction of Tinto's theoretical model.

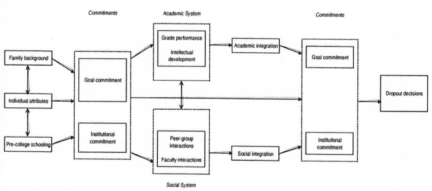

Figure 2. A Conceptual Scheme for Dropout from College

Though far from complete, much of the empirical research on student departure from college provides support for Tinto's theoretical explanation (Bean, 1980; Bean & Metzner, 1985; Nora, 1987; Pascarella & Terenzini, 1983; Strayhorn, 2005). However, results are not completely conclusive as some studies do not support Tinto's initial conceptualization (Munro, 1981; Williamson & Creamer, 1988). In fact, recent critics argue for a complete reworking of Tinto's theoretical model, especially when studying students at non-residential commuter campuses (Braxton, 2000b). Despite these contradictions, the weight of evidence shows that Tinto's model has been used extensively in studying college student departure (Pascarella & Terenzini, 2005) and his model has served well to enhance our knowledge of the "student departure puzzle" in higher education.

For this reason, I elected to use Tinto's (1993) model in my study of African American male attrition. His model provided a theoretical lens through which the central phenomena—dropping out of college—could be understood. In the next section, I describe how Tinto's model was employed and where and in what ways the theoretical framework affected my study.

Effects of the Framework on My Study

Recall that the purpose of this study was to estimate the influence of various factors in attrition for Black men in college. Measuring these relationships was made possible by designing the study using Tinto's theoretical model as an organizing scheme. That is, the theoretical orientation set forth by Tinto guided the entire research process.

Building the Argument

First, Tinto's theory of student departure from college was immeasurably useful in building the argument for the study. Much of Tinto's work centered on the fact that somewhere between 40-60 percent of all college students drop out of school before earning their degree. In fact, research shows even higher attrition rates among specific subpopulations of students. Though not directly related to this study, research has shown that first-year students tend to drop out at exceedingly high rates (Bank, Biddle, & Slavings, 1990; Fidler, 1991; Tinto, 1993). That is, nearly half of all "leavers" depart before the start of their second year. Specifically, Tinto (1987) found that approximately 75 percent of those students who depart will leave during the first two years of college, the greatest proportion in the first year.

Tinto (1993) and others have provided evidence that student attrition rates are even higher among those who face unique and uncertain challenges in college. African American men represent such a group of students. Black men—in and out of college—are often characterized by disparaging terms, such as endangered, uneducable, dysfunctional, incorrigible, and dangerous, that perpetuate negative stereotypes (Ferguson, 2000; Gibbs, 1988; Majors & Billson, 1992; Parham & McDavis, 1987). These stereotypes, in turn, can negatively impact their achievement and "threaten" (Steele, 1997, 1999) Black male behavior (Bailey & Moore, 2004). Furthermore, these challenges, without support, may impede or thwart their pursuit and attainment of the American Dream (Hochschild, 1995) and influence the fact that African American men often experience difficulty in educational spheres (Jackson, 2003; Jackson & Crawley, 2003; Moore, Flowers, Guion, Zhang, & Staten, 2004).

In many ways, these difficulties are inextricably linked to the central constructs of Tinto's theoretical framework. For example, a miscellany of scholarship and research on African American men in college provides evidence that Black men are more likely to experience the *most* academic and social challenges in college as compared to any other group (Flowers, 2003; Hrabowski, Maton, & Greif, 1998; Jackson, 2003; Jackson & Crawley, 2003; Steele, 1997). Given their small enrollment numbers, the low proportion of Black men on campus can impact the social climate and *social integration* of such students into the fabric of college life. Similarly, challenges faced at other points throughout the educational pipeline contribute to what Cuyjet (1997, p. 6) calls the "underpreparedness" of Black men. These issues can have a deleterious effect on the degree to which Black men become connected to or members of the academic realm of college (i.e., academic integration).

Armed with these theoretical statements, I built my argument around the fact that recent reports published by the U.S. Department of Education indicate that Black male enrollment rates have failed to keep pace with other racial/ethnic subgroups. The under representation of Black men in college, combined with their challenges in society at large, may undermine their efforts to integrate academically and socially, which, in turn, affects their ability to persist to degree attainment. Central tenets of Tinto's theory helped me to narrow the focus of the study as well.

Focusing the Study

The theoretical framework also guided the focus of my study by sensitizing me to the factors that affect college student retention. Influences on college student retention are many and range from demographic to academic factors, variables that can be easily manipulated and those that are, for all intents and purposes, fixed (e.g., race, gender), and both internal and external motivations. To narrow the study's scope, I drew upon Tinto's (1993) interactionalist theory of college student departure and focused only on those variables identified in his model. Recall that Tinto identifies a number of important predictors of student retention: student's pre-college attributes, individual goals and commitments, and academic and social integration into college life, to name a few. This set boundaries (or "delimits") around my study as I sought to operationalize pre-college background attributes (e.g., age, race), individual goals (e.g., degree goals), and commitments (e.g., the extent to which participants felt committed to their current institution). Indeed, there are other factors that could have been considered but Tinto's theory allowed me to justify my decision to focus on these factors in particular. The theoretical framework influenced other aspects of the study, including the development of the leading research questions.

Developing the Research Questions

Since I narrowed my focus to factors identified by Tinto (1993) in his model of college student retention, theory allowed me to ask questions about such factors (e.g., pre-college traits, institutional and goal commitments) *and* helped me to understand that such questions were connected to the very issue of student retention. In other words, I could ask "to what extent pre-college traits influenced academic integration," realizing that academic integration, according to Tinto's model, was a precursor of student retention. Without theory, I may have struggled to see how and if these two constructs were related and, when taken together, represent a piece of the "departure puzzle" (Braxton, 2000a).

Selecting Relevant Variables

The purpose of this study was to measure the influence of college experiences on African American males' decision to stay in or depart from college. To this end, Tinto's (1993) model proved to be a powerful tool for selecting relevant variables. Theory allowed me to examine the influence of students' background traits, pre-college experiences, initial commitments, and levels of academic and social integration on the decision to leave college. Moreover, his theoretical proposition attempted to explain the relationship among these variables in the decision making process. This is an important characteristic of theory (Anfara & Mertz, 2006); theory should explain something. So, I used theory as a heuristic tool for making decisions about the study's main variables.

According to theory, external commitments are related to college student retention. That is, whether and the extent to which students have commitments *external* to campus life yields a noticeable influence on the likelihood of "staying in" or "leaving" college. So, I operationalized external commitments using several variables such as marital status, assuming that married students may have greater external commitments than single students, and the degree to which work affected one's schoolwork. Not only did the theoretical framework employed in this study justify these decisions but prior research also supported the selection of these variables. For instance, Nora and Cabrera (1993) tested different indicators of institutional commitment including loyalty to one's institution; this is consistent with other researchers (Hatcher, Kryter, Prus, & Fitzgerald, 1992; Okun & Finch, 1998).

Guiding Data Analysis

The theoretical model of college student departure was posited to be hierarchical and temporal (Tinto, 1993). That is, Tinto originally believed that students' background traits and initial commitments to his or her institution and degree plans influenced the degree to which the student acclimated to the academic and social life of college. Then, one's level of academic and social integration affected subsequent commitments to college and ultimately influenced the decision to persist.

The order and timing of Tinto's theory guided my data analysis. To model the direction and nature of the theoretical framework, I employed sequential or hierarchical, binomial logistic regression procedures to analyze data from the nationally representative sample of Black male collegians. This technique allowed me to force-enter variables in the model based on a priori theory (Keith, 2006). This approach was used in my previous research (Strayhorn, 2005, 2006a) on retention.

Interpreting Findings

The primary purpose of this study was to measure the influence of selected factors (e.g., pre-college, academic, non-academic) on the decision to stay in college. Multivariate analyses of longitudinal data from African American men attending 4-year institutions were conducted. The longitudinal data permitted the introduction of statistical controls for an extensive battery of confounding variables and allowed me to model closely the direction of Tinto's (1993) interactionalist theory of college student departure, which served as the study's theoretical framework. Results suggest several important conclusions.

First, findings present evidence that background traits have a significant effect on the decision to stay in college. Parent's level of education was statistically significantly related to students' persistence in college. For example, students whose parents had lower levels of education (e.g., high school diploma only) were significantly less likely to persist to degree than students whose parent's attained higher levels of education (e.g., college degree or advanced).

Second, this study provided evidence that high school academic achievement, as measured by high school grade point average (GPA), had a statistically significant impact on one's persistence in college. In this study, persistence was not simply a function of background traits such as parent's level of education. Persistence was a function of the linear combination of several independent variables including high school GPA. In fact, the statistically significant positive effect of GPA persisted in the presence of an array of control variables. This implies that high school GPA explains the variance in persistence above and beyond one's background traits.

Finally, results suggest that the effect of these variables on persistence may not be consistent for all Black men. For example, younger African American men had a lower predicted probability of persisting in college than older Black men. This may underscore an important consideration in examining college impacts—namely, conditional effects. As Cruce, Wolniak, Siefert, and Pascarella (2006) said: Given the increasing diversity of American undergraduates, we should expect conditional effects of this type to be "the rule rather than the exception" (p. 379). Tinto's theoretical explanation of the persistence/retention process allowed me to "see" what needed to be discussed in the findings section of my report. Specifically, I gave attention to the key concepts included in his model (i.e., pre-college/background traits, initial commitments, academic and social integration, subsequent commitments, and external influences) and the role they play in predicting student retention.

Closing Thoughts

Indeed, Tinto's interactionalist theory of college student departure provided a means to understand the complexities of student persistence/attrition. Yet, it is important to note that Tinto's theory is one of many ways in which the student departure puzzle can be studied. Theoretical frameworks, such as the one employed in this study, allow researchers to see in new and different ways what seems to be ordinary and familiar. By the same token, they allow the researcher to "see" certain aspects of the phenomenon while concealing other aspects. This is an important point to remember and provides a motive for using alternative or multiple frameworks to study this same issue in the future.

Theory played at least one other important role in the study. It provided clues about new or existing programs and services that could be useful in increasing retention rates among Black men. And even these implications had academic and social roots. For instance, I advocated for the establishment of summer bridge programs and continued support for federal TRIO programs, based on the study's findings. In this way, theory was the "glue" that seemed to connect each individual part of the manuscript—the introduction, the literature review, methodology, findings, and discussion. Drawing on theory was immeasurably useful in studying student drop out, as it provided constructs for "talking about" dropping out of college, as Astin (1975) said, as well as clues for "doing something about" college student attrition.

Chapter Three

Choosing Frameworks, Choosing Colleges

"A student's college choice is the result of a complex re-
lationship between individual agency, family cultural
capital, and the structure and organization of the school
to which the student adds the influences of friends, the
family's financial situation, an after-school job, as well
as numerous other influences."
(McDonough, 1997, p. 111)

In Chapter Two, I outlined two trends that characterize the nature of higher education in the United States. Recall that a hallmark of the American system of higher education is reflected in the diversity of its institutional types (Lucas, 1994). And, according to the 2000 Carnegie classification system, there are approximately 600 liberal arts colleges, 600 comprehensive universities, and nearly 2,000 community colleges in the United States. Research universities are yet another type of institution and there about 260 such campuses in the nation (Carnegie Foundation for the Advancement of Teaching, 2000); universities can be further classified into two categories of institutional control (e.g., public and private) and campus type (e.g., predominantly White institutions, historically Black colleges and universities, Hispanic-serving institutions, tribal colleges) (Strayhorn & Hirt, 2008).

The diversity of American colleges and universities is further complicated by the diversity of students enrolled in college today. While colonial college students were sons of wealthy, White statesmen and religious leaders largely (Thelin, 2004), today's college student population consists of more women than men and more racial/ethnic minorities than ever before (U.S. Department of Education, 2006).

McDonough (1997) further explained that approximately 60 percent of all high school seniors enroll in one of nearly 4,000 colleges in the

U.S. system of postsecondary education. Indeed, this figure suggests an opportunity structure that is egalitarian and "meritocratic" (p. 1) generally. Yet, she contends "society's opportunity structure does not work equally well for all" (p. 1). Aggregated rates mask important and glaring disparities in access between White students and students of color, men and women, as well as between upper and lower socioeconomic status (SES) students. For instance, while upwards of 75 percent of White and upwards of 80 percent of high-SES high school graduates enroll in some form of postsecondary education immediately after graduation, only about 35-50 percent of African Americans and 33 percent of low-SES students do so (Adelman, 2002; Gándara, 2002). And, when they do enroll, African Americans and other non-Asian racial/ethnic (e.g., Latinos) and economic minorities tend to be concentrated at minority-serving institutions (Strayhorn & Hirt, 2008); less selective 4-year institutions, and 2-year community colleges (Baum & Payea, 2004; Ellwood & Kane, 2000; Thomas & Perna, 2004).

With these trends in mind, I became curious about the extent to which students' pre-entry attributes and social class status influence the college destinations of students. Specially, I wanted to understand the degree to which gender, race, and class (as measured by socioeconomic status) influence students' college choices and whether adding these factors to traditional econometric "choice models" (i.e., those considering availability of aid, cost) increased the explanatory power of the original model. After reading McDonough's (1997) book, *Choosing Colleges*, and scouring through the literature on college choice and studies that suggest that attending a more selective institution yields greater benefits and social status attainment (Karabel & Astin, 1975; Sewell, 1971; Velez, 1985), I narrowed my focus to students' sociodemographic backgrounds and choice of a selective university. This was the gap addressed by the study upon which this chapter is based.

The Study

To illustrate the use of college choice theory as a guiding framework in studying the influence of gender, race, and socioeconomic status on the college choice decisions of first-year students, I refer to my large-scale survey study published in the *NASAP Journal* (Strayhorn, 2006d). In this study, I used data from a nationally representative sample of 3,924 students enrolled at 28 selective, postsecondary institutions nationwide. Specifically, I conducted secondary data analyses on information drawn from the National Longitudinal Survey of Freshmen (NLSF), a sample consisting mostly of students enrolled at the "top 50" institutions in the country as ranked by the U.S. News and World Report (Massey, Charles, Lundy, & Fischer, 2003). A single question guided this study: To what extent do gender, race, and SES influence the college choice of students attending selective institutions?

Using hierarchical multinomial logistic regression techniques, I found that gender, race, socioeconomic status, and an array of other determinants influence college choice outcomes of college students at selective institutions. Odds ratios revealed a number of interesting relationships. "The odds are greater for an individual whose mother completed post-graduate studies to attend a private research university over a public institution," and "being female significantly increases the odds of attending a liberal arts college over a public research institution" (Strayhorn, 2006d, p. 107). Interestingly, African Americans were more likely to attend a public research institution (versus a private research university or liberal arts college) than any other racial/ethnic group; this finding is consistent with previous research (Hearn, 1984, 1990). Considering the type of institutions involved in this national study, this finding suggests that African Americans are more likely to attend large, public research universities (e.g., state land-grant colleges) than private research universities like Harvard and Princeton, controlling for all other differences. In consonance with prevailing college choice theories, I also found that the college destinations of NLSF students were statistically related to the quality of their high school (McDonough, 1997) and correlates of SES such as parents' income level (Gándara, 1995; Hearn, 1987).

The Theoretical Framework

Early on, I realized the need for a theoretical framework to guide my study of the college choice process. For instance, I wondered, "What is the dependent variable in college choice studies?" Several ideas came to mind including a dichotomous variable indicating whether an individual enrolled in college or not. Another idea focused on institutional control, which is generally defined as public versus private. Neither of these seemed appropriate as the study's purpose centered on institutional selectivity. Thus, I turned to the literature and theory on college students' decision-making processes.

Indeed, college choice is a complex process. And, the literature on college choice is extensive, psychological and sociological, as well as noticeably dated—much of it dates back over 40 years ago. For instance, some scholars focus on the role that academic factors such as institutional reputation (Dixon & Martin, 1991) and program availability (Anderson, 1994) play in the decision-making process (e.g., Alwin & Otto, 1977; Boyle, 1966).

Yet another line of inquiry emphasizes the extent to which economic and financial considerations shape the college destinations of students. Availability of financial aid (Jackson & Chapman, 1984; Spies, 1978) and cost (Murphy, 1981) are major considerations in econometric studies. However, economic models are limited in their power to explain the college destinations of students as a major assumption of such models is rarely met. That is, economic models assume that students have complete or near complete information to make decisions that maximize utility through simple cost-benefit analysis. Since most students make decisions about college without access to complete information, other models or theoretical notions are needed to augment our understanding of this complex process. With this, I turned again to the college choice literature to identify factors related to students' decisions.

A plethora of studies exist on the ways in which students choose one college over all other "options." For instance, countless studies have shown that academic achievement is the most powerful predictor of college attendance (Adelman, 1999; Alexander & Eckland, 1975; Hearn, 1991) and students with high academic achievement in high school are more likely to attend 4-year institutions (Hossler, Braxton, & Coopersmith, 1989; Litten, 1982; Zemsky & Oedel, 1983). Yet, I struggled to understand how each factor was organized in the students' decision-making scheme overall and how students thinned their choices over time. So, I developed a matrix of the prevailing college choice theories; these are summarized in the sections below.

"Deciding to attend a college is generally considered a stage-wise process in which students start with a list of higher education opportunities available to them. Then, students narrow their choice based on relevant information" (Strayhorn, 2006d, p. 103). Lastly, students refine their perceptions, values, and subjective assessments of their objective probabilities (Bourdieu, 1977b; MacLeod, 1995) and choose a single institution, as described in a number of existing postulations (Freeman, 2005; Gilmore, Spiro, & Dolich, 1981; Hossler, 1985; Hossler & Gallagher, 1987; Jackson, 1982; Kotler, 1976; Kotler & Fox, 1985; Litten, 1982).

The most widely cited theory on college student choice was developed by Hossler and Gallagher (1987). They proposed a three-phase model of student college choice consisting of three qualitatively distinct stages in students' decision-making process: predisposition, search, and choice. Predisposition refers to students' pre-entry attitudes and preferences toward attending college. These dispositions are formed early and nurtured over one's childhood. In this phase, students make a decision between attending college and alternative status or economic attainment paths such as working or military service (Hossler, Schmit, & Vesper, 1999).

Search is the second stage of the model, which refers to a period of data collection in which students gather information about various colleges to develop a "consideration set" (Hossler et al., 1999, p. 146). Sources of information span the gamut from parents and siblings, to guidance counselors and college fairs. The final stage is choice where students vet their viable options and choose a particular college after comparing the social and academic attributes of their entire set.

Traditional college choice models are limited in explanatory power given that *different* students consider *different* factors when choosing *different* colleges. Models that incorporate social constructs and students' characteristics may have more explanatory power than those that include individual perspectives only (Hossler et al., 1989; Perna, 2000). Thus, I employed a combined conceptualization of college choice to measure the impact of gender, race, and SES on students' decisions, controlling for an extensive array of intervening variables. The theoretical orientation powerfully influenced the nature of my study.

Effects of the Framework on My Study

When I set out to conduct this study, I realized the need to understand how college choice was defined both theoretically and conceptually. I mentioned earlier that I read (and re-read) McDonough's (1997) *Choosing Colleges* and Freeman's (2005) *African Americans and College Choice* during the summer before I started this study; I was already quite familiar with Hossler and Gallagher's (1987) outline of the student choice process. Armed with this information, I started to conceptualize the study and the theoretical framework shaped my thinking at each stage.

Building the Argument

The first thing I learned from the research and theory on college choice is that "college choice is a complex process" (Strayhorn, 2006c, p. 100). Somewhat surprising to me, I learned that there had been quite a few "college choice" studies published since the 1970s; indeed, many of these were dated at the time of my writing and relatively few focused on issues of race, gender, and class or SES, with few exceptions (Terenzini, Cabrera, & Bernal, 2001).

So, after talking about the general direction of college choice research, I argued for my study by highlighting the gaps in our literature in terms of how race, gender, and class influence college choice decisions. For example, I wrote: "In fact, some studies suggest that attending a more selective institution yields higher benefits and social status. Yet, few studies focus on students' sociodemographic backgrounds and choice of a selective institution" (Strayhorn, 2006c, p. 101).

In addition, I learned that there were several critiques of existing college choice frames. For instance, Perna (2000) pointed out that traditional college choice models are essentially based on simple economic reasoning (i.e., rational choice) and (a) students rarely have complete information to make true cost-benefit comparisons and (b) college choice is a bit more quirky and idiosyncratic than most rational choice models allow. So, I used this information to advance my argument for studies that take into account additional factors:

> ...such models are limited in explanatory power given the fact that few students have complete information to identify the advantages and disadvantages associated with attending one institution over another. Other models referred to as 'status attainment' models have been preferred to explain college choice as a function of family conditions, socialization processes, and external influences. (Hossler et al., 1999, p.103).

Focusing the Study

In this study, I used data from the restricted-use data file of the National Longitudinal Survey of Freshmen (NLSF), provided through Princeton University. The NLSF consists of hundreds of variables reflecting information collected via a baseline survey in 1999, face-to-face interviews, and a follow-up survey in 2000-2001. Trying to narrow the scope of a study with so much information available is a daunting task; the theoretical framework was a useful heuristic for whittling down the size of the database.

Given that one of my central independent variables was race, I decided to use the entire study sample (N = 3,924) consisting of 998 White students, 1051 African American students, 916 Hispanics, and 959 Asians. In addition, I wanted to focus on gender-related effects; thus, it proved beneficial that 58 percent of the sample were women.

Hossler and Gallagher (1987) called attention to several sources of influence on one's college decisions including experiences that might "predispose" someone to college attendance. With this in mind, I studied the database to find proxies for experiences or opportunities that might encourage students to consider college early on. I settled on several variables which the database allowed me to operationalize; I will say more about this later in the chapter. Once I developed a set of research-based factors, which are purported to influence one's college choice, I developed measures for race, gender, and class. These decisions clarified the focus on my study and led me to revisit my research question.

Developing the Research Questions

Originally, I had a purpose statement and "implied" research question in mind. Namely, the purpose of the study was to estimate the influence of race, gender, and class on college choice for students attending the nation's selective colleges. However, theory and research allowed me to see that there are multiple factors that influence one's college choice decisions and these factors may complicate the influence of sociodemographic factors such as race, gender, and class. For instance, several scholars (Hearn, 1984; McDonough, 1997) stress that high school academic performance and "curriculum" play a role in determining one's college destination. For instance, if students do not have access to high quality college preparatory coursework (e.g., Algebra, advanced science courses) in high school, his/her postsecondary options are constrained, if not limited, to less-selective institutions, 2-year community colleges, and vocational schools.

With this understanding, I revised my original purpose statement and adopted a single research question that took into account my main independent variables and other potentially confounding factors:

The purpose of the present study is to explore the relationship between gender, race, SES, and college choice using a national sample of college students who attend selective institutions. Specifically, this study examines the background traits, academic preparation, and achievement of college students to determine the impact of background factors on college choice, controlling for an extensive array of intervening variables.... A single question guides this study: To what extent do gender, race, and SES influence college choice of students attending selective institutions? (p. 101)

Selecting Relevant Variables

Using information from the theory and research on college choice, I identified several proxies, which the database allowed me to operationalize, for experiences and opportunities that might predispose students to college attendance. For instance, parent's level of education was included in this analysis based on the premise that students whose parents attended college may inherit certain values about higher education that predispose them to attending college upon high school graduation (Hagedorn & Tierney, 2002; Villalpando & Solórzano, 2005). In addition, research shows that students of color tend to be influenced powerfully by their relatives during the college choice process (McDonough, antonio, & Trent, 1997).

Secondly, Freeman (1997) examined the ways in which Black students from different socioeconomic backgrounds perceive and make meaning of barriers to attending college. She found that some Black students, especially those from racially segregated high schools and neighborhoods, fear being isolated on predominantly White campuses; she coined this the "intimidation factor." To estimate the influence of this factor, I included a set of predictors that measured one's high school composition (e.g., percent Black, percent Hispanic).

Finally, several variables were included in the analysis based on the fact that academic preparation significantly increases or inhibits one's chances to attend selective colleges. As shown in the published article, I included measures of high school type (e.g., public, private, home) and number of years respondents took certain high school courses (e.g., chemistry, trigonometry). These courses are deemed college preparatory courses upon which admission counselors look favorably (Tierney, Corwin, & Colyar, 2005), thereby increasing one's chances of being admitted to a selective college.

Guiding Data Analysis

College choice, according to the study's central theoretical perspective, consists of three sequential phases. In consonance with the framework, I planned for data analysis to proceed in three stages. First, descriptive statistics would allow me to observe the relative proportion of students in selective liberal arts, research universities, and private institutions. Second, cross-tabulations and exploratory correlation analyses would provide rough estimates of the direction and strength of associations between race, gender, class, and other variables included in the analysis. Finally, I needed an analytic procedure that would allow me to regress 14 sets of independent variables on a single, categorical dependent variable. The dependent variable was defined by three discrete categories—liberal arts college, public research university, private research university—thus, "multinomial logistic regression [was] the analytical technique of choice (Pampel, 2000)" (Strayhorn, 2006d, p. 105).

Interpreting Findings

The outcome of college choice theory is the students' actual choice—that is, the type, level, selectivity, or identity of the institution students choose to attend. Thus, I decided to report descriptive findings by race and institutional type. For instance, a larger proportion of African Americans attended public research universities (30 percent) than any other racial/ethnic group. However, the largest proportion of Asian students attended liberal arts college (26 percent), perhaps surprisingly.

Second, although the purpose of the study was to estimate the influence of race, gender, and class on college choice decisions for students attending selective colleges and universities, I remained curious about the study's implications for future theory. That is, I wanted to know whether a model that included sociodemographic variables, predisposition factors, and measures of academic preparation for college was "better suited" for predicting students' choices. Indeed, I found strong support for this hypothesis:

> *Hierarchical multinomial logistic regression results*
> *suggest that adding race, [gender], and SES improved*

the explanatory power of the college choice model. The change in deviance (-2 log likelihood) associated with the addition of [such factors] suggests a statistically significant improvement in fit. (Strayhorn, 2006c, p. 106)

Finally, recall that I struggled initially to understand what the dependent variable would, should, or could be in a study on college choice. Was it whether or not the student chose a college? If so, where is the variance in a sample of students enrolled in college such as the student samples provided in most large, national databases (e.g., Baccalaureate & Beyond, NLSF)? Or, was it a continuous outcome variable (e.g., number of institutions to which students apply)? Neither of these seemed an appropriate "choice" for the purposes of my study. Indeed, theory provided clues that the outcome variable was likely a dichotomous variable (i.e., mutually exclusive categories that require a true choice over other options). And, with this in mind, I analyzed data using multinomial logistic regression procedures and presented findings in terms of probabilities and odds ratios. For instance, I found that the "odds are greater for an individual whose mother completed post-graduate studies to attend a private research university over a public institution" (Strayhorn, 2006c, p. 107); that is, the odds are 1.48 times higher for such individuals.

Closing Thoughts

Theory was critically important to this quantitative investigation of the college choice process. Hossler and Gallagher's (1987) three-stage model of college choice served as the prevailing theoretical framework but indeed their work was augmented with a number of other empirically-based perspectives (Freeman, 1999; McDonough, 1997; McDonough et al., 1997). Theory shaped the argument for the study, the purpose statement and research questions, variable selection, data analysis, and even the way in which results were presented in the final report.

Still a number of important directions for future research should be pursued. For instance, in my study, college choice was operationalized to reflect one's decision to attend a selective liberal arts college versus a public or private research university. Future researchers might employ logistic regression procedures to study differences in the college decision-making process for students attending 2-year versus 4-year public or private institutions. While some scholars might devote attention to understanding differences in the factors considered when choosing a historically Black college or university (HBCU) versus a predominantly White institution (PWI) among African American collegians, others might study the college choice process of White students at Black institutions. Such information can be instrumental in increasing racial/ethnic diversity at HBCUs, if necessary, and may provide clues to supports that assist White students in Black college contexts.

While useful, Hossler and Gallagher's (1987) college choice model has rarely been used completely in research. Said differently, scholars tend to describe the theory without using or operationalizing all of its central constructs. Future researchers should use large, nationally representative samples and locally collected survey data to create additional measures of predisposition, search, and choice. In fact, I suggest that we, as researchers, take a bit of time to observe, interview, or interact with students and their families to identify the various ways in which students are predisposed to college throughout their youth. For instance, both of my kids spend enormous amounts of time with me at home, at work (i.e., University), and even at conferences; I imagine that these experiences powerfully predispose them to college (and an academic career). Though anecdotal, my son's consistent proclamation lends support to my suspicion: "When I grow up, I want to go to college. And, I'm going to the University of Tennessee, Knoxville" (my former institution). There may be other ways in which students are predisposed to college attendance that remain unapparent, unexamined, unidentified, and therefore, misunderstood. Secondly, if my son is right that he will attend the University of Tennessee (or The Ohio State University), then future researchers might pay attention to other ways that students foreclose on a certain college early on (e.g., during college visits, legacy status, peer influence). We simply do not know enough about how these experiences operate in the college choice process. Indeed, I encourage future researchers to use existing or develop new frameworks for studying why students choose colleges.

Chapter Four

Understanding Challenges, Seeing Supports: Using Sanford's Theory with Black Males

"Environments that provide a combination of challenge and support tailored to students' level of development are recommended to assist students in adapting appropriately to the challenges they encounter"
(Chickering, 2004, p. 117).

It has been said that if you see a turtle perched on a treetop, you can rest assured that he had some help getting there. Similar wisdom can be used when studying the experiences of college students, especially historically underrepresented minorities such as students of color who face significant challenges throughout the educational pipeline. Empirical research, some of which is my own, has shown that some students of color—for example, African Americans—attribute their success, in part, to strong supportive networks of parents, siblings, teachers, counselors, and mentors to name a few. For instance, parents tend to play a role by assisting students with homework (Massey et al., 2003) and in helping their student resolve some of the problematic conditions that African Americans face as they negotiate their way through the educational pipeline (Heath & McLaughlin, 1987; Hrabowski et al., 1998).

The problem is further complicated when studying the experiences of Black male collegians who confront additional stressors and unique obstacles in social and educational settings (Bailey & Moore, 2004; Gibbs, 1988; Kunjufu, 1986; Noguera, 2003; Polite & Davis, 1999). For example, "Black men are often viewed as an at-risk population in education (Bailey & Moore, 2004; Davis, 2003; Moore, 2000) and tend to be described with words that have negative connotations such as uneducable, endangered, dysfunctional, dangerous, and lazy" (Strayhorn, 2008e, p.

27). Assigning such negative labels to Black men is problematic because disparaging words can perpetuate and reinforce negative stereotypes. Indeed, there are other factors that may limit the success of Black men in higher education.

Some Black men lack information about college readiness and the college application process (Freeman, 2005; McDonough et al., 1997; Polite & Davis, 1999). For instance, Polite studied 115 Black males enrolled at Metropolitan High School and uncovered that teachers and counselors often fail to encourage Black men to consider college prep opportunities such as a advanced math courses. Furthermore, parents of Black boys often lack a college education and the requisite academic "know-how" to assist their son *to* and *through* college (Hrabowski et al., 1998).

As a result, the enrollment of Black men in higher education has flat-lined or, in some cases, declined in recent years (U.S. Department of Education, 2006). Most racial/ethnic subgroups have seen significant progress in their postsecondary enrollment, while there has been little to no progress in increasing participation rates among Black men over the last quarter of a century. Today, Black men represent the exact same proportion of total undergraduate enrollment as they did in 1976—less than 5 percent (Mortenson, 2001; Strayhorn, 2008e).

Despite clear and consistent evidence that these challenges and startling trends persist over time, we know comparatively little about supportive mechanisms that enable the success of African American male collegians. The handful of studies that address this issue are predominantly qualitative (Berry, 2005; Bonner, 2001; Hamilton, 2005; Harper, 2003) and based on small samples ranging from two to thirty-two men. Thus, quantitative studies based on larger samples of Black men are warranted and the study, upon which this chapter is based, was designed with this gap in mind.

The Study

The study, *The Role of Supportive Relationships in Facilitating African American Males' Success in College*, sought to "add a missing component to the student success literature base by applying quantitative methods to a relatively large sample of Black men to test the importance of supportive relationships on grade point average and satisfaction with college as correlates of retention" (Strayhorn, 2008e, p. 29). The stated purpose of the study was to measure the relationship between academic achievement (as measured by grades), satisfaction with college, and students' supportive relationships with major socializing agents on campus. Three research questions guided the analysis: (a) What is the relationship between supportive relationships and academic achievement in college for Black men? (b) What is the relationship between supportive relationships and satisfaction with college for Black men? (c)What is the relationship between supportive relationships and satisfaction with college, controlling for a battery of potentially confounding factors?

To investigate this topic, I conducted secondary data analyses on information drawn from the 2004-2005 national administration of the *College Student Experiences Questionnaire* (CSEQ), which has been the focus of several studies featured in this volume. Specifically, I restricted the sample to African American men only. These sampling criteria yielded 231 respondents. A majority were freshmen (51 percent), 15 percent were sophomores, 20 percent were juniors, and 15 percent were seniors.

Applying a combination of descriptive and multivariate statistical techniques, I found that supportive relationships were statistically associated with Black males' satisfaction with college but not grades. Additionally, results indicated that this relationship persists in the presence of a fairly rigorous set of statistical controls; accounting for approximately 16 percent of the variance in student satisfaction. That is, Black men who reported frequent and meaningful supportive relationships with others on campus were more satisfied with college than their peers with fewer and/or less meaningful interpersonal relations. And this finding held true for Black men with similar personal and academic histories—indeed, supportive relationships seem to facilitate student success in college. Previous theoretical formulations about college student development informed my inquiry (Strayhorn, 2008e).

The Theoretical Framework

Sanford's (1962) notions of challenge and support served as the conceptual framework for this investigation. In college environments, challenge refers to encounters with new situations, people whose background differs from one's own, and ideas that cause cognitive dissonance (Festinger, 1957) or stimuli for cognitive growth and development (Creamer & Associates, 1990) Support, on the other hand, refers to aspects of the human and material environment that provide students with security, confidence, sense of belonging (Hurtado & Carter, 1997), and information needed to succeed (Rogers, 1961). Sanford's explanation posits that academic and social development is a function of challenges in the environment balanced by a sufficient level of support. One way support is provided to students is through meaningful interpersonal relationships with major socializing agents on campus including one's peers, staff, and faculty members (Pascarella & Terenzini, 2005). Therefore, it seemed reasonable to assume that supportive relationships may influence student satisfaction with college. The study was designed to test this hypothesis for African American males.

Effects of the Framework on My Study

The overarching framework influenced the study in a number of ways and this will be addressed in the sections below.

Building the Argument

Scholars who study African American males in educational settings approach the problem from a number of different angles. For instance, some authors (e.g., Fries-Britt, 1997; Harper, 2003) talk about the fact that most research on Black collegians, especially academically gifted students, is based on a deficit perspective—that is, how much Black students lack and the impact of such shortages on their academic success. Still others identify the long-term social ramifications of problems faced by Black men early on in the educational pipeline (Davis, 2001; Polite & Davis, 1999). In the article upon which this chapter is based, I organized the statement of the problem around the prevailing framework—challenges and supports.

In the opening paragraphs, I used the literature to illustrate several challenges faced by African Americans, especially Black men, in pK-12 and higher education. For instance, I outlined that "educational outcomes of African American students are not on par with those of their White and Asian counterparts" (Strayhorn, 2008e, p. 26). As another example, I highlighted that Black male youth often face challenges when trying to access college preparatory curricula (Polite & Davis, 1999), overcome negative stereotypes about Black men (Bailey & Moore, 2004), and "level the playing field" in terms of future earnings (Strayhorn, 2008c). Thus, I concluded that, without support, such challenges might compromise the satisfaction and subsequent success of Black male collegians.

Meaningful interpersonal relationships with individuals upon whom Black men can rely for encouragement and guidance are one type of "support." By organizing the *problem statement* around the theoretical framework, I was able to narrowly focus the study on Sanford's (1966) main concepts.

Focusing the Study

Recall that Sanford (1966) posited academic and social development as functions of challenges in the environment balanced by a sufficient level of support. This formula also served to focus the study on specific aspects of the college experience. That is, academic and social development were operationalized as academic achievement (i.e., academic development) and satisfaction with college (i.e., social development). I used the conceptual framework to make important decisions about the study. For instance, I could have measured academic development using proxies for perceived intellectual development, as measured by the CSEQ (Strayhorn, 2008a), course credit accumulation, or even major choice (Malgwi, Howe, & Burnaby, 2005). Sanford's explanation seemed to justify my selection of grades and satisfaction.

Not only did Sanford's (1966) definition of challenge and support seem to undergird my focus on academic achievement and satisfaction with college, but it also helped me to settle on the important role that meaningful interpersonal relationships play in facilitating student success. Sanford explained "supports" as aspects of the human and material environment that provide students with security, support, and a sense of belonging. In that way, I wanted to focus on aspects of the *human* and/or *material* environment. Certainly, financial factors such as student aid and social psychological factors such as motivation and self-efficacy determine students' success in college. But there are other aspects of the *human* and/or *material* environment such as interpersonal interactions. By focusing on Sanford's model, I "saw" the opportunity to examine the influence of interpersonal relationships on Black male students' success. And, that revelation led me to ask specific research questions.

Developing the Research Questions

Writing research questions for this study was a matter of both science and art. It was science in the sense that I was developing a fairly rigorous empirical research project. As a result, my variables needed to be specified clearly, the sample needed to be reflective of the study's purpose, and the methods for data analysis needed to be appropriate given the study's database. On the other hand, it was like art in that I only needed to blend together various aspects of the conceptual framework to develop my research questions. Consider Sanford's definition: academic and social development $(Y') = f$ [challenges (X_1) + supports (X_2)]. Thus, three research questions were developed using the formula (Strayhorn, 2008e, p. 30): (a) What is the relationship between supportive relationships and academic achievement in college for Black men? (b) What is the relationship between supportive relationships and satisfaction with college for Black men? (c) What is the relationship between supportive relationships and satisfaction with college for Black men, controlling for differences in background (i.e., age, marital status, classification, parent's education, aspirations) and college grades? The research questions, then, provided clues for selecting relevant variables.

Selecting Relevant Variables

The dependent variable in this study assessed students' satisfaction with college. To operationalize student satisfaction, I drew upon previous research and existing theoretical formulations (Bean, 1980). Satisfaction was defined as "the favorability of a students' subjective evaluation" of college (Elliott & Shin, 2002, p. 198). So, I sought CSEQ items that seemed to elicit students' opinions about college. I settled upon two items; one of which asked "how well do you like college?" After testing the psychometric properties of this hypothesized scale, I created a summated scale by adding the two items. Originally, each item was placed on a 4-point response scale. Thus, response options for the summated scale ranged from 2 ("not at all satisfied") to 8 ("very much satisfied").

A second outcome variable measured students' academic achievement in college. Response options ranged from 1 ("C, C-, or lower") to 5 ("A"). College grades often serve as a proxy for academic integration in college, as hypothesized by Tinto (1993).

Lastly, I sought a reliable measure of the frequency and nature of students' supportive relationships with others on campus, in consonance with prior research and Sanford's (1962) notion of support. Specifically, I sought survey items that seemed to reflect the ways in which major socializing agents assist students through college. An example of this scale was worded, "Talked with a faculty member or staff member about personal concerns." Response options ranged from 1 ("never") to 4 ("very often"). Theory helped me make decisions about variables to include in this analysis. Similarly, theory shaped my plans for data analysis.

Guiding Data Analysis

Perhaps Sanford's (1966) definition is described best as a conceptual, rather than theoretical, model. This distinction among terms is often overlooked or reduced to nothing more than mere semantics. However, I believe these two terms *can* refer to different tools. While theoretical frameworks are often characterized as sets of "interrelated constructs, definitions, and propositions that present[s] a systematic view of phenomena..." (Kerlinger, 1986, p. 9), conceptual frameworks offer a relatively simple definition or explanation of a concept that might otherwise be considered too abstract or too ordinary to apprehend.

Sanford's (1966) work held significant assumptions about the interrelationships among variables included in the study. For instance, supports were presupposed to be related to academic achievement and satisfaction; therefore, I conducted exploratory correlation analyses to test for such linkages. To measure whether supports influenced satisfaction above and beyond background characteristics and grades, I conducted hierarchical linear regression analyses. By accounting for potentially confounding variables, I adjusted the estimates of effect downward, thereby increasing the ability to isolate a true, net effect of "supports." Once data were analyzed, I was left to interpret the findings. Looking back, I "see" how the overarching framework influenced my interpretations both consciously and subconsciously.

Interpreting Findings

In the article, I stated that the consequences of challenges faced by Black men in educational settings are nontrivial and serious. Without support, such challenges tend to compromise the academic success of Black men in college and often lead to dissatisfaction with college. Since dissatisfaction is an important predictor of and precursor to leaving college, at least theoretically (Bean, 1982; Tinto, 1993), it seems reasonable to assume that both challenges and supports are related to retention. Challenges, on the one hand, increase the odds of dropping out of college prematurely, while supports reduce the odds of leaving college before completing one's degree. In this way, theory allowed me to interpret the findings of this study in light of a consequence, a critical policy issue in higher education, and to connect this analysis to a broader literature on college student retention. Why was this important?

In terms of policy, I was able to "see" how this study informed institutional and individual efforts to reduce attrition rates. By focusing efforts on increasing and improving supportive relationships with others on campus, administrators could effectively alter dropout rates by raising retention rates. This clarified the implications for federal, state, and institutional policy. Additionally, theory illuminated strategies that could be employed to facilitate such relationships (e.g., advising, mentoring, faculty-in-residence programs), thereby increasing Black male students' satisfaction with college.

Lastly, notice that one of the first interpretations made in the "Discussion" section of the manuscript focuses on theoretical implications. I wrote, "That having a strong support person(s) was positively related with satisfaction in college for Black men [and that] has theoretical significance" (Strayhorn, 2008e, p. 36). Specifically, the study's findings lend support for using Sanford's (1966) work in future studies on African American males in higher education. For instance, future researchers might employ Sanford's notions to understand whether *certain* types of support (e.g., financial, social) ameliorate *certain* types of challenges (e.g., transition, social adjustment) more than others. Alternatively, results provide support for using other theoretical frameworks that attempt to explain social interactions (e.g., social exchange theory [Blau, 1964]) or socialization of individuals (Weidman, 1989).

Closing Thoughts

To bring the article full circle, I ended with several statements about additional challenges faced by Black students in general and Black male collegians in particular. For example, I pointed out that some Black students experience isolation and alienation on campus due to the lack of a critical mass of peers and Black faculty/staff upon whom they can rely for support. Racism and discrimination are other challenges. And all of these factors may influence the ease with which students establish meaningful interpersonal relationships with peers and faculty members, for example. Thus, increasing the number of Black faculty members, personnel, and students on campus is an important and necessary step toward increasing the success of Black male students in college.

I followed similar logic when identifying additional supports in the implications section. For instance, I named several "constituencies who have a vested interest in improving student satisfaction with college or raising retention rates..." (Strayhorn, 2008e, p. 39). Groups ranged from directors of student success centers to provosts, enrollment management professionals to housing staff members. Even though campus administrators may not be able to remove all the challenges that Black men face in a timely manner, they can provide appropriate supports to improve Black males' odds for success in college. Employing Sanford's (1966) theory to study Black male collegians can enrich one's understanding of the challenges they face and the supports they need to succeed in college. By taking into account the "hills and valleys he come through [*sic*]," we are better positioned to "measure him right" and help him through college.

Chapter Five

College Impact Theory and Academic Achievement of First-Generation Students

*"If there was ever a time when we needed a broad rep-
ertoire of approaches to inquiry in research on the impact of college, it is now"
(Pascarella & Terenzini, 1998, p. 155).*

My doctoral dissertation focused on graduate student persistence. I analyzed data from the *Baccalaureate and Beyond Longitudinal Study* (B&B: 1993/1997) to estimate the validity, as it were, of prevailing retention theories when studying graduate versus undergraduate students. I was struck by the virtual absence of graduate students from the literature on college student retention, attrition, and success. Despite a handful of unpublished dissertations, reports, chapters, and monographs, most of what was known about college student retention focused exclusively on undergraduate students. Of course this was "good news" on one hand, as it made easy my attempts to articulate the gap that my study was designed to fill. On the other, it required me to read both bodies of literature to build a foundation for my work, thereby doubling, if not tripling, the amount of research I had to master.

I can remember vividly jotting down notes about factors that influence student outcomes, namely retention. And, it was then that I ran across a full discussion of Terenzini, Springer, Yaeger, Pascarella, and Nora's (1996) college impact model. Zeroing in on the role of pre-college characteristics, as outlined in the college impact model, and comparing it to Tinto's (1993) retention framework, I began puzzling over the experience of students whose parents did not attend college—that is, first-generation college students.

In typical "Terrell fashion," I followed my own curiosity *to* and *through* dozens of published studies on first-generation college students (e.g., Terenzini et al., 1996). I learned that first-generation students (FGs)represent approximately 30 percent of all college enrollments in the United States. While many more first-generation students enroll in college today, thanks to a number of successful efforts to broaden access for historically underserved groups (Tierney & Hagedorn, 2002), FGs are still less likely to graduate from college within 8 years of high school completion (Choy, 2001; Ishitani, 2003). A confluence of factors may lead to low attainment rates among first-generation college students including limited advice and information about postsecondary education (Bowman & York-Anderson, 1991); little to no support from family and friends in the college decision-making process (Pratt & Skaggs, 1989); and difficulty balancing family, friends, and educational demands (London, 1989). I surmised that these challenges may inhibit the ability of first-generation college students to manage the academic demands of college, which, in turn, could affect one's grades.

Picking up where my "search" left off, I scoured the literature for information about academic achievement of first-generation college students. Despite some agreement among scholars about the academic performance of first-generation college students, there were a number of mixed results that seemed to warrant additional research. Some research suggests that FGs earn lower grades in college than their peers (Billson & Terry, 1982); others suggest that first-generation college students earn grades similar to their non-FG peers (Inman & Mayes, 1999; Strage, 1999). Curious and confused, I decided to investigate this issue more closely using a nationally representative sample of students.

The Study

In this chapter, I draw upon a study published in the *NASPA Journal* (Strayhorn, 2006b) to illustrate use of college impact theory. Using data from the *Baccalaureate and Beyond Longitudinal Study* (B&B:1993/1997) conducted by the National Center for Education Statistics, I conducted multivariate analyses "to measure the impact of first-generation status on academic achievement in college" (p. 86). The weighted analytic sample consisted of 1,019,000 individuals; Eighty-three percent of the sample was White, the majority was female (53 percent), and the mean age was 18.57 ($SD = 3.03$).

A summary of the study and its key findings are reflected in the abstract shown below:

First-generation college students face a number of unique challenges in college. These obstacles may have a disparate effect on educational outcomes such as academic achievement. This study presents findings from an analysis of the Baccalaureate & Beyond Longitudinal Study using hierarchical multiple regression techniques to measure the influence of first-generation status on cumulative grade point average (GPA) in college, controlling for pre-college and college variables. Findings suggest that first-generation status is a significant predictor of GPA controlling for an extensive array of background and intervening variables. Initially, background variables accounted for a small but significant proportion of college GPA variance. Final results suggest that first-generation status significantly explains differences in cumulative GPA, accounting for nearly 22 percent of GPA variance. Findings are congruent with college impact theory and support prior conclusions. Still, a number of important relationships and implications for future research are discussed. (Strayhorn, 2006b, p. 82)

The Theoretical Framework

After reading the books and published studies on first-generation college students to which I alluded earlier, I was left wanting to know more. I set up three conversations (of course, over coffee) with undergraduate students who self-identified as first-generation college students. Topic of our conversation? Their academic achievement. And, specifically, to what or whom they attributed their success (or lack thereof). These conversations proved to be enormously helpful in shaping my initial thoughts about the research and, subsequently, drove my decision to adopt college impact theory as the guiding framework.

Most of the students described themselves as "determined," "focused," "motivated," and "involved" in college. Despite some challenges and setbacks, my cast of interviewees rated their performance as successful. They attributed their success to studying long hours, juggling multiple tasks at once, and having the support of individuals on campus, to name a few. Thus, choosing college impact theory was a relatively easy decision as it provided constructs for talking about these concepts and the various ways in which they affect student outcomes.

College impact theory consists of three stages, which reflect movement from students' college expectations through transition between high school (or work) and college onward to the impact of college on educational outcomes such as achievement and degree attainment. The model is, by definition, longitudinal and reflects conceptualizations found elsewhere (Astin, 1984; Pascarella & Chapman, 1983).

Six key concepts characterize college impact theory: pre-college traits, curricular patterns, in-class experiences, out-of-class experiences, institutional context, and learning outcomes. Examples of pre-college traits range from performance on admissions tests to demographic factors. College experiences include both in- and out-of-class activities. Institutional context taps aspects of the campus environment and prevailing ethos; variables used in previous studies range from institutional selectivity to control (i.e., public vs. private). Lastly, student outcomes include learning, academic achievement, retention, and even learning in specific domains such as critical thinking, effective communication, and appreciation of diversity. Table 5.1 outlines college impact theory and provides a list of variables included in the study.

Effects of the Framework on My Study

College impact theory influenced the study in several ways and these will be addressed in the sections that follow.

Building the Argument

The theoretical framework starts with entry into college. In keeping with the model, I started to build the argument for the study around issues of access to higher education and moved quickly to identify the pre-college backgrounds of my targeted population. Consider this excerpt from the opening paragraph:

> In recent years, access to higher education has been improved for traditionally underserved and underrepresented groups of students. This expansion of higher education in America has resulted in increasingly higher proportions of women and racial/ethnic minorities enrolling in college

than has been seen in previous decades (Pascarella & Terenzini, 2005). Another group that benefits from recent
shifts in access to college is students whose parents did not
attend college. . (Strayhorn, 2006b, p. 82)

Since college impact theory posits that experiences (i.e., involvement, successes, challenges) affect student outcomes, I organized the
literature review around the unique challenges that first-generation college students face. In that way, theory helped to narrow my focus.

Table 5.1
Conceptual Model of College Impact Theory

Background traits	Pre-college factors	College factors	Dependent variable
Age	ACT score	Major	Grades
Sex	SAT score	Work	
Race	2-year attendance	Remedial	
	Delayed enrollment	Educational goals	
		Personal aspirations	
		Academic & social integration	
		Time-to-degree	
		HBCU status	

Note. ACT = American College Test. SAT = Scholastic Aptitude Test.
HBCU= Historically Black college or university.

Focusing the Study

After reviewing the literature, I noticed an interesting feature of most published studies on first-generation college students. With few exceptions, most of the studies were descriptive and sought to describe the personal and educational histories of students whose parents did not attend college (e.g., Choy, 2001). Comparatively few studies focused on the extent to which academic and social experiences of first-generation students affect outcomes such as grades. Theory permitted mse to see this hypothesis as possible. It also provided an outline for the literature review section.

First, I talked about the challenges that first-generation students face in terms of access and laid the foundation to "drop anchor" on the study's purpose. Weaving together a set of studies, I narrowed the scope of the study to first-generation college students; highlighted the fact that FGs are disproportionately represented among racial/ethnic minorities and economically disadvantaged families; circumscribed the study to academic and social aspects of college life; and, reported the blurring confusion about FGs and college grades.

Using the "mixed results" as fuel to move to the purpose, I wrote: "The purpose of this study is to explore differences in the influence of various factors on the academic achievement of first-generation and non first-generation students" (Strayhorn, 2006b, p. 84). This led me to the research question or questions.

Developing the Research Questions

In its original form, the study consisted of four separate research questions—one addressing each of the four factors (i.e., background, pre-college, academic, and social). Thanks to an anonymous reviewer, I reduced the set of questions to a single research question, which, at least according to the reviewer, seemed to resonate better with my overarching theoretical framework. The main research question was (Strayhorn, 2006b, p. 84): *What influence do background, pre-college, and college characteristics have on academic achievement for first-generation and non-FGs?*

Theory was not only useful for reducing the number of research questions to one, but it also provided language to refer to sets of variables that, according to research, may influence first-generation students' academic achievement. For instance, I included three measures of background traits, four pre-college factors, and many more college factors.

Without the aid of theory, the research question would have been interrupted by a long list of predictors: *What influence do age, sex, race, ACT score, SAT score, 2-year attendance, delayed enrollment, major, work, remedial courses...(and the list goes on)...have on academic achievement for first-generation and non-FGs?* College impact theory provided a way of clustering variables together in sets (e.g., background). Not only did theory help me cluster variables together but it guided my selection of relevant variables in the first place.

Selecting Relevant Variables

Consistent with other large-scale secondary data analyses like my dissertation and those presented in this volume, I knew early on that I would have to make decisions about which variables to include in the analysis. College impact theory gave me clues about "which" variables to include—that is, I sought measures that relate to each stage of the theoretical framework. While useful for drawing the broad brushstrokes of the analysis, I still had to identify appropriate survey items and proxies for the factors included in the model. For instance, the *Baccalaureate and Beyond Longitudinal Study* provides a good number of background traits including gender, race, and age. Another benefit of the database is the inclusion of information about students' academic histories. Drawing upon college impact theory, I argued that these indices (e.g., ACT score, SAT score) are proxies of pre-college factors (e.g., preparation for college). Once I had selected variables that were relevant for the study, I organized them into sets according to the overarching framework. Throughout this process, I constantly reflected on my plan for data analysis.

Guiding Data Analysis

College impact, according to theory, consists of three stages, as mentioned earlier. To model this design, I planned for data analysis to proceed in three stages. First, descriptive statistics would allow me to see any observable patterns in the independent and dependent variables. Second, exploratory correlation analyses would provide cursory estimates of the direction and magnitude of associations amongst variables. Finally, I decided to use hierarchical linear regression (HLR) to analyze these data.

HLR is "a method of regression analysis in which independent variables are entered into the equation in a sequence specified by the researcher in advance. The hierarchy (order of the variables) is determined by the researcher's theoretical understanding of the relationships among the variables" (Vogt, 1999, p. 129). HLR was the analytic technique of choice as it allowed me to (a) model college's impact as a sequential process and (b) force-enter variables in three, sequential blocks following the order outlined in the modified theoretical model.

Interpreting Findings

Theory shaped my interpretations of the study's findings in several ways. First, I started this work with an interest in college impact theory's ability to explain disparities in student outcomes. Based on the results of the analysis, I concluded that the revised or modified version of the college impact model is useful for explaining GPA variance. I found that "cumulative GPA was a function of the linear combination of independent variables from all three sequential models" (Strayhorn, 2006b, p. 97). In this way, I made sense of the findings by comparing my results to the guiding framework.

Related, I found that being African American and first-generation exerted statistically significant effects on achievement in the face of statistical controls. In other words, even among those who share similar backgrounds and academic histories, African Americans and first-generation college students perform differently in college. For instance, White women earn significantly higher grades than Black men in this analysis. So, I advocated for "the revision and expansion of traditional college impact models that may be limited in examining multicultural issues and outcomes that are influenced by individual traits or settings" (Strayhorn, 2006b, p. 98). Significant policy and practice attention should be paid to the experiences of those who live at the intersection of multiple margins such as African American first-generation collegians.

Closing Thoughts

Alas, I end where I began. This chapter opened with a clarion call for a broad(er) "repertoire of approaches to inquiry in research on the impact of college" than is currently available (Pascarella & Terenzini, 1998). While useful for the featured study, college impact theory may be limited in its applicability to historically underrepresented students (e.g., first-generation students) and racially/ethnically diverse individuals. Consequently, I urge future researchers to consider "trying on" alternative lens to study this same issue. For instance, theories from social psychology (e.g., self-esteem, self-efficacy) may be helpful in understanding the role that individual motivations and agency play in determining students' success. Other variables might be incorporated into existing theories to test whether they act as mediators or moderators of presently known effects. For instance, using information presented in Chapter 7, future researchers might expand or revise college impact models to include resilience, self-authorship, or aspects of context. Future work might also test the relevance of prevailing theories (e.g., retention, college impact) to first-generation students' experiences using a side-by-side comparative approach. For example, I can envision a study that uses the same sample, same data to determine whether Tinto's (1993) retention theory, Astin's (1984) involvement theory, or some version of college impact theory is most powerful for predicting college grades. Using a smooth blend of descriptive statistics, correlations, and comparisons of parameter estimates and model fit indices (e.g., R^2), researchers might break new ground on the impact of college on students and just how best we can measure its effect.

Chapter Six

Sentido de Pertenencia: Interrogating Sense of Belonging for Latino College Students

"Latina/o students' perceptions of a hostile climate directly affect their sense of belonging in their colleges" (Castellanos & Jones, 2003, p. 8).

A few years ago, during an invited guest luncheon for the College Student Personnel (CSP) master's degree program in which I teach, I enjoyed a side-by-side casual conversation with the university's Provost about student retention rates in general and at our institution in particular. With a background in Germanic language and history, the Provost spoke about "student success" factors without references to the literature upon which most of his arguments stood. On the contrary, it was clear that he had a keen understanding of the campus culture and how work gets done within various academic units. With expertise in student retention research and theory, I sprinkled my comments with parenthetical-like references to Bean (1982), Tinto (1993), Astin (1993), Braxton (2000c), and the student success literature, some of which was my own, that provided empirical support for my assertions, but lacked the necessary experience with our campus to suggest the degree to which theory-based programs and interventions would be successful at UT, if properly implemented. Indeed, we made a likely team—the consummate practitioner-scholar duo. A few weeks later, the Provost invited me to serve as his special assistant and I graciously agreed. In that role, I would conduct campus-wide research studies and assessments of students' experiences, author and disseminate findings to campus constituencies (e.g., deans, heads, faculty, and students), and use the campus as my "laboratory" (R. Holub, personal communication, January 30, 2007).

As Special Assistant to the Provost, I have used my "laboratory" to study the experiences of first-year students at a large, public research university; African American males at a predominantly White institution, and even high-achieving minority students who, according to research, would be considered "at risk" (U. S. Department of Education, 2000). In addition, I have had the opportunity to meet and know many students who continue to be an important source of inspiration—students like Vincent. Consider Vincent's narrative when asked "How often do you think about your race at [said] university?" He replied:

> *I think about my race all the time; it's constantly there...mostly because there are so few Latino students and faculty on campus. Usually when you hear the word diversity, you're not talking about Latina/os. We're rarely talked about. I do all I can to fit in...I'm involved in a couple of groups on campus and we're trying to get a new Latino fraternity started on campus. But that's hard work and it can distract from other stuff like study-ing, writing your papers [laughing], and focusing on your work to graduate and get out of here. I really do try but at the end of the day I know it's not for me...like it's not my campus. [What do you mean by 'not your cam-pus?'] Well, like I just don't fit in and don't always feel like I belong here....*

After reading through transcripts from this project, I became inter-ested in *sense of belonging* as a theoretical construct, an antecedent to student retention, and its relation to the experiences of racially and ethni-cally diverse students at predominantly White institutions. Scouring the literature for references to sense of belonging, I ran across multiple cita-tions to Hurtado and Carter (1997). Thus, I thought that would be a promising point of departure for reading about sense of belonging and understanding how it operates in the lives of Latino collegians. Accord-ing to Hurtado and Carter, sense of belonging "contains both cognitive and affective elements in that the individual's cognitive evaluation of his or her role in relation to the group results in an affective response" (p. 328). Specifically, they were interested in understanding how social in-teractions enhanced student's affiliation with college.

The Study

Armed with a general understanding of sense of belonging and its theoretical underpinnings, I returned to "Vincent's story" that opened this chapter. Vincent's words left me curious about Latino students' sense of belonging and its relation to other critical issues in higher education. I wondered: What influence interactions with diverse peers have on sense of belonging for Latino students? And, whether the influence was more or less compared to their White counterparts? These questions led to the study upon which this chapter is based.

The Theoretical Framework

To understand the relationship between academic and social experiences and Latino students' sense of belonging, it was necessary to identify sources that provided information for talking about these constructs. For the reasons listed above, it made sense to employ Hurtado and Carter's (1997) explanation of sense of belonging as one of the guiding frameworks for the analysis. Their frame provided a lens to "see" aspects of sense of belonging that might otherwise seem unclear or remain hidden. For instance, they point out that sense of belonging consists of both cognitive and affective elements, which not only called my attention to the academic and social determinants of sense of belonging but could also be used to justify inclusion of variables from both domains in this analysis.

To augment my understanding of the potentially unique interplay between academic and social experiences in college, I leaned upon Tinto's (1993) interactionalist theory of college student departure as a guiding framework as well. Briefly stated, Tinto theorized that student traits form individual degree goals and institutional commitments, which interact over time with collegiate experiences (both informal and formal) to influence one's decision to leave college. His theory emphasizes the role that involvement in the academic and social systems of college life plays in predicting students' departure decisions. Melding these two perspectives together, it seemed reasonable to assume that involvement with others on campus, especially interactions with diverse peers, may influence one's sense of affiliation, membership, or sense of belonging on campus.

Effects of the Framework on My Study

Theory allowed me to "see" in new and different ways what might otherwise appear blindly abstract or unambiguously familiar. In other words, without the aid of theory, I could have puzzled over sense of belonging to no end. On the one hand, it appears too complex to distill its constituent elements (e.g., cognitive and affective evaluations). On the other, sense of belonging could be erroneously equated with satisfaction or involvement. Indeed, it is different. Theory influenced the study in other areas.

Building the Argument

If one outlines the opening argument that was framed for this analysis (see Strayhorn, 2008d), it can be divided into academic and social justifications for giving additional attention to sense of belonging among Latino collegians. For instance, the opening sentence reads, "College participation rates have increased for all groups over the past 30 years. However, significant gaps across racial/ethnic groups persist" (p. 301). Not only are Latino students disproportionately represented among college enrollees, but they also are (a) largely concentrated at either Hispanic-serving, less-selective, or 2-year institutions (Nora, Rendón, & Cuadraz, 1999; Thomas & Perna, 2004); (b) less likely to complete their college degree when compared to their White and Asian peers, and the rest (c) take longer to complete their degree, on average (Swail, Cabrera, & Lee, 2004). Finally, some research suggests that some Latino students are un- or underprepared for the rigor of college courses (e.g., Warburton, Bugarin, & Nunez, 2001). All of these are academic-related issues.

Next, the argument shifts to social factors that influence Latino collegians' success. For instance, I argue that differences in the amount and nature of sociocultural capital inherited by Latino students may limit or expand their opportunity for success in academic settings. A number of scholars believe that students of color inherit different forms of sociocultural capital than that which is valued and rewarded in school settings (Carter, 2005; Villalpando & Solorzano, 2005). Consequently, students of color are forced to acquire the capital necessary to succeed in such settings, representing a "second curriculum" which they must master (Fleming, 1981).

Indeed, there are other social factors that I considered to assemble my argument for the study. Since these are fully explained in the article, I will resist the inclination to be repetitive and merely cite a few examples. Other social factors include: strong familial obligations, feelings of isolation, marginalization, and self-defeating stereotypes. Stereotypes, I argue, have a social dimension that is important to note when studying the influence of students' interactions with diverse others—namely, stereotypes are formed in the absence of face-to-face interactions (Sigelman & Tuch, 1997).

Focusing the Study

The theoretical framework provided reasonable justification for bringing together many important ideas that narrowed the focus of this study. For instance, the focus on academic factors seemed to imply that the sample might differ in terms of academic preparation for college and grades in college. Consequently, the sample consisted of Latino and White collegians with varying levels of achievement rather than a more homogenous subgroup (e.g., high-achievers).

The emphasis on social factors also narrowed the scope of this study. Students have countless social experiences in college ranging from involvement in clubs and organizations, studying in groups, working out in the gym, and even socializing with faculty outside of class (Pascarella & Terenzini, 2005). Although all of these have been shown to be related to student success in college with varying degrees of importance, it was necessary to focus on a specific form of social interaction. By focusing on interactions with diverse peers, the scope of the project was narrowed to a manageable breadth and the initial research questions were recorded although in need of slight revision.

Developing the Research Questions

As a scholar of color, the primary goal of my research is to improve higher education for the benefit of diverse college students in a variety of contexts. In many ways, I study the experiences of historically underrepresented groups in higher education because of my own experiences in college. Thus, through my work I attempt to interrogate my own college experiences from a critical stance typically using quantitative methods (Stage, 2007a). This approach might be best described as critical inquiry, which renders me a "quantitative criticalist" (Stage, p. 1).

My biography empowered me to consider a number of prevailing theories with the healthy dose of skepticism that each deserves. For instance, I was aware that Tinto's (1993) theory enjoys near paradigmatic stature (Braxton, 2000) but seems to have limited applicability to the decisions of students of color, such as African Americans and Latinos. In fact, some scholars (e.g., Rendón, Jalomo, & Nora, 2000) have criticized Tinto's conceptualization for its assimilationist language and assumptions—that students must break ties with former communities to become integrated into the academic and social communities of campus. For some students—especially students of color in predominantly White environments—severing supportive relationships with members of one's culture of origin can lead to serious psychological issues, dissatisfaction, and academic failure (Guiffrida, 2004, 2005; Strayhorn, 2008e; Thomas, 2000).

As a result, I consciously employed an alternative conceptualization (i.e., sense of belonging) that focuses on perceived membership and "fit" rather than integration. Additionally, I consciously chose questions that seek to challenge the dominant paradigm. Rather than focusing on factors associated with Latino collegians' *integration* into college environments, I asked, "What is the relationship between academic and social experiences in college and *sense of belonging* for Latino students attending 4-year colleges and universities?" A second question focused on differences or inequities that may exist between Latino students and their White peers. My epistemological stance (i.e., quantitative criticalist) combined with the guiding theoretical frame called into question the existing theory and assumptions about Latino students' success, thereby compelling me to ask the typical *answer* (e.g., Latinos lack the integration necessary to succeed) a different *question*.

Selecting Relevant Variables

The purpose of the study was to estimate the relationship between Latino students' college experiences and their sense of belonging on campus, operationally defined using items from the College Student Experiences Questionnaire (CSEQ). To this end, the two theoretical perspectives proved to be powerful tools for selecting relevant variables. For instance, Tinto's (1993) retention theory and research about Latino collegians' success in college identified academic and social factors purported to be related to students' sense of belonging or sense of membership in campus life. Academic factors included: year in school, grades, transfer status, time spent studying, and working with a faculty member on research. Social variables included: involvement in clubs and organizations, working on campus, working off campus, living on campus, and most central to the study, interactions with diverse peers (Chang, 2001).

The dependent variable in this study was developed to reflect students' sense of belonging, as delineated by the conceptual framework (Hurtado & Carter, 1997). Specifically, I operationalized sense of belonging using three items from the CSEQ that are believed to have psychometric and qualitative properties that are consistent with prevailing definitions of sense of belonging and previously used measures (e.g., Gonyea, Kish, Kuh, Muthiah, & Thomas, 2003; Hoffman, Richmond, Morrow, & Salomone, 2002-2003; Hurtado & Carter, 1997). That is, I created a composite measure of sense of belonging using three survey items that were deemed to be related to the global construct; an example of this scale is, "Thinking of your own experience, rate the quality of your relationships with other students."

To understand whether the CSEQ provided information that could be used to operationalize sense of belonging, it was necessary to read extensively across diverse disciplines including social psychology, cultural theory, sociology, and philosophy, to name a few. In addition, I conducted a comprehensive literature review of all recently published studies (i.e., within last 5 years) on sense of belonging using a myriad of electronic databases (e.g., ERIC, EBSCO). Focusing on studies where sense of belonging appeared in the title, abstract, or body only, I uncovered over 500 books, chapters, journal articles, reports, and conference papers. Then, I narrowed the list by excluding those that did not fit the sampling criteria (e.g., recent publication) and all conference papers since they are rarely available for public use.

Reviewing the literature led to several conclusions that later informed the selection of and the way in which I operationalized the dependent variable. First, while there is general consensus about the important role that sense of belonging plays in the success of college students (Hausmann, Schofield, & Woods, 2007; Hurtado & Carter, 1997; Johnson et al., 2007), there is considerable disagreement about its definition. Prevailing definitions are varied and problematic. For instance, sense of belonging has been defined as: (a) a feeling of connectedness, or a feeling that one is important to others (Rosenberg & McCullough, 1981; Taylor, Turner, Noymer, Beckett, & Elliott, 2001); (b) perceived support from peers and faculty (Hoffman et al., 2002-2003); (c) a sense of community (d) a psychological sense of school membership (Goodenow, 1993); and (e) "the extent to which students feel like accepted, respected, and valued part of their academic context" (Freeman, Anderman, & Jensen, 2007, p. 208). While, in most cases, evidence exists to support disparate conceptualizations, these conflicting and often contradictory definitions are too confusing and vague to be helpful for science or practice. So, in this study, I was greatly aided by the narrow focus of Hurtado and Carter's (1997) definition and the database upon which analyses were based.

Guiding Data Analysis

Similar to the study of retention outlined in Chapter Two, the order and timing of Tinto's (1993) theory guided by data analysis in part. For instance, recall that Tinto's model was posited to be hierarchical and temporal. That is, he hypothesized the direction of relationships (e.g., direct, indirect) and the order in which variables influence one another. He originally believed that background traits determine initial commitments and degree goals, which, in turn, influence the degree to which students become acclimated to the academic and social life of college.

Based on this understanding, I conducted hierarchical regression tests with a nested design to estimate the net effect of various sets of predictors (namely, interactions with diverse peers) on Latino and White collegians' sense of belonging, controlling for differences in potentially confounding background traits such as age, gender, and parent's level of education. Hierarchical regression was employed in consonance with the theoretical framework. Hierarchical regression is a "method of regression analysis in which independent variables are entered into the equation in a sequence specified by the researcher in advance" (Vogt, 1999, p. 129).

Interpreting Findings

After conducting analyses of data drawn from the College Student Experiences Questionnaire, I was left to interpret these findings in light of the overarching theoretical framework and prior research. Generally speaking, results suggest a number of important findings. For instance, White students ($M = 16.30$, $SD = 3.14$) reported a higher sense of belonging than Latino students ($M = 15.78$, $SD = 3.56$), on average. This lends support to previous research about disparities in educational outcomes among White and Latino college students (Arbona & Nora, 2007; Massey et al., 2003). Findings from this analysis indicate that Latino students also feel a lower sense of belonging at predominantly White campuses than their White peers. It may be the case that academic and social struggles (e.g., limited English proficiency, social isolation, and racism) limit the extent to which Latino students develop a sense of belonging on campus (Justiz & Rendon, 1989; Oliver, Rodriguez, & Mickelson, 1985). Indeed, more information is needed to unpack the underlying causal mechanism.

Secondly, hierarchical linear regression results suggest two important findings. That the model accounted for more of the variance in sense of belonging for Latino students ($R^2 = 11$ percent) than White students ($R^2 = 9$ percent) provides evidence to support several theoretical and methodological approaches. For instance, these results add supportive evidence to the literature that sense of belonging may be a more culturally relevant way to measure minority students' "connectedness," "attachment," or "membership" to campus. Indeed, the study calls into question pre-existing theories that focus on integration while supporting alternative explanations such as sense of belonging.

In terms of methodology, the analysis upon which the present chapter is based provides empirical support for analyzing survey data using a comparative group approach, where appropriate (Carter & Hurtado, 2007); that is, a "method of conducting statistical analyses separately by group" (p. 29). Future researchers should consider this recommendation when designing future studies, especially those based on applying critical approaches to conventional quantitative research. This approach is appropriate when testing whether the influence of independent factors, X's, on a dependent variable, Y, in Group A is more or less than that observed in Group B. If this is not the purpose of the study, there is no reason to make a comparison group (e.g., Whites) the norm by which all others are measured.

Closing Thoughts

In closing, both Tinto's (1993) interactionalist theory of college student departure and Hurtado and Carter's (1997) definition of sense of belonging were gainfully employed in this study of Latino students' academic and social experiences in college. Theoretical understandings, such as the ones used in this study, allow college impact researchers to see in new and different ways what might otherwise be seen as ordinary and familiar (Anfara & Mertz, 2006). I've started to say that theory is a way of exoticizing the ordinary (Besnier, 1995) or making the familiar strange (Jakobson, 1987). And while useful, all theories have limitations.

Consequently, future researchers are encouraged to consider identifying and using alternative explanations to study this same issue. Theories such as social networks theory, ecological systems theory, and social cognitive theory may represent promising directions for expanding this line of inquiry.

Turning back to Vincent's story that opened this chapter, results from this multivariate analysis have implications for policy, practice, and research. Much of this is outlined in the published article. Indeed, findings may provide clues to levers that can be used to increase Latino students' sense of belonging on campus, which, in turn, may raise retention rates and increase the number of Latino students who complete their college degree.

Chapter Seven

Theoretical Frameworks in College Student Research: Conclusions

"If you have built castles in the air, your work need not be lost; that is where they should be. Now put the foundation under them."
–Henry David Thoreau, *Walden*

Throughout this volume, I have attempted to explain the pervasive effects of theory on college student research, both directly and by example, using my own published research as a sort of curriculum. Specifically, each chapter was designed to address what a theoretical framework is, how it can be used in college student research, and how it affects such research. I "zeroed in" on theory's role in *building the argument, focusing the study, developing the research questions, selecting relevant variables, guiding data analysis,* and *interpreting findings.* In this way, the book was designed to make the implicit explicit, to help novice and seasoned researchers "put the foundation" under their work, to reveal many aspects of the research process, especially those that pertain to the important role of theory, that are often hidden and rarely discussed publicly. To do this, a general definition of theory was needed.

Recap of Theory's Definition

Drawing upon information from a number of sources including students' comments, anecdotes from colleagues, published research articles, and Anfara and Mertz' (2006) *Theoretical Frameworks in Qualitative Research*, I noticed a confusing array of definitions about theory and/or theoretical frameworks, all varying in scope and character. For instance, some scholars refer to conceptual frames (Merriam, 1998); propositions (Argyris & Schon, 1974); abstract categories (LeCompte & Preissle, 1993); conceptual maps (Ausubel, 1963; Strauss, 1995); models (Parker,

1977); stances (Crotty, 1998); postulations (Astin, 1984); constructs (Kearney & Hyle, 2006); typologies (Douglas, 1982; Harris, 2006); hypothesized relationships (Lewin, 1936; Sanford, 1962); organizing observations (M. Jones, personal communication, June 15, 1999); theoretical orientations (Henstrand, 2006); interpretive tools (Geertz, 1973); lenses (Henstrand); and even roadmaps (Kearney & Hyle). While these metaphors are powerful devices for understanding the important role that theory plays in empirical research, the sheer number of descriptors can be misleading and blur the meaning of theory. Under this cover, theory generally referred to plausible explanations of observed phenomena (Strayhorn, 2006c).

With this operational definition in plain view, it is implied throughout the book that theory enhances the rigor of a study by linking together in a logically, connected whole what might otherwise be seen as random, isolated facts. And it is the simple connections across complexities that signify rigor. By drawing upon theory, studies can be based on systematic knowledge rather than on hunches, anecdotes, and improvisation.

Theory has other effects on college student research. For instance, sometimes higher education researchers, especially those who work "on the frontline" or "in the trenches" (i.e., practitioner-scholars), can be so local in their orientation to a problem that connecting the research to a broader issue is difficult and, thus, generalization is virtually impossible. As demonstrated several times in this volume, theory can provide the scaffolding necessary to link a research topic (e.g., relationships) to a critical issue (e.g., retention) in higher education.

Lastly, theory afforded me opportunities to feel some wonder about topics, many of which were the focus of previous research. In other words, theory allowed me to "see" the topic in new and different ways; this was particularly helpful in identifying "the gap" or what qualified my work as a "new contribution." For instance, retention theory provided clues about the ways in which background traits and collegiate experiences might coalesce over time to influence student departure decisions. This sensitized me to the experiences of African American males in *certain* campus contexts (e.g., 4-year institutions) and led to several studies, one of which is described in an earlier chapter of this volume. In some cases (see Chapter 6), I used theory "to exoticize the ordinary" (Besnier, 1995, p. 560); "to make the ordinary strange" (Jakobson, 1987, p. 25). For all its benefits, I should note one caveat about theory's impact on research. While theory offers new and/or complex "ways of thinking" and "ways of seeing" (Morgan, 1986, p. 12) some things, it also tends to conceal others. One way to work around this limitation of theory is to become familiar with and use multiple theories in college student research. With this in mind, let us turn now to a brief summary of the theories presented in earlier chapters.

Summary of Theories Discussed

In Chapter 1, I described sets of theories that can be used in college student research ranging from psychosocial theories of college student development to college impact theory. Recall that psychosocial development theory is a guide for understanding student learning and maturation in college. For instance, Kohlberg (1969) posited three levels of moral reasoning: pre-conventional, conventional, and post-conventional. And each level represents a qualitatively distinct understanding of the relation between self and society. Later in the opening chapter, I frame a discussion of sociocultural capital (i.e., social and cultural capital) as defined by leading sociologists (Bourdieu, 1977a; Coleman, 1988). Chapter 2 illustrated how I applied Tinto's (1993) theory of college student retention to identify longitudinal determinants of retention among African American males at 4-year institutions. Chapter 3 focused on my study of first-year students at highly selective colleges and universities, which was based upon Hossler and Gallagher's (1987) college choice model. They proposed a three-phase model of student decision-making: predisposition, search, and choice.

Next, I used ecological systems theory to examine the influence of families and schools on student behavior (Chapter 4). Chapter 5 provided an example of applying *challenge and support* theory (Sanford, 1962) to study the extent to which supportive relationships with major socializing agents affect Black males' achievement and satisfaction with college. College offers a number of challenges for students, which often lead to disequilibrium or cognitive dissonance. The repertory of coping strategies that students bring with them to college may be insufficient for such challenges, thereby catalyzing the process of growth and development. To manage such challenges, students need support; one form of support is meaningful interpersonal relationships with others on campus. Indeed, I found evidence that supports tend to mediate challenges and increase student success. In Chapter 6, I referred to a study in which sense of belonging (Hurtado & Carter, 1997) served as the theoretical lens from and through which I looked at Latino students' experiences in college. Sense of belonging refers to the extent to which students feel "part of" a campus community; it contains both cognitive and affective elements. I found it to be a useful heuristic for studying Latino students at 4-year institutions, the majority of which were predominantly White. Though far from complete, the main chapters of this text offer readers some understanding of about 14 theoretical frameworks. Table 7.1 provides an overview of the theoretical frameworks mentioned in this volume.

Other Examples of Theory in Practice

College student researchers are encouraged to search for other theoretical frameworks and to think beyond the theories presented in this single volume. Indeed, countless examples of theory in practice abound. For instance, college student researchers might examine closely a scholarly journal that requires, explicitly or implicitly, authors to identify a theoretical framework. Such journals include the *Journal of College Student Development, The Review of Higher Education,* and *The Journal of Higher Education.* For instance, in Volume 49, Number 4 of the *Journal of College Student Development,* Baxter Magolda (2008) describes three elements of self-authorship: trusting the internal voice, building an internal foundation, and securing internal commitments. Drawing on earlier work (Kegan, 1994), Baxter Magolda defines self-authorship as the internal capacity to define one's beliefs, identity, and social relations (p. 269). In that same volume, Cole and Espinoza (2008) used cultural capital and cultural congruity theory to ground their study of Latino students in science, technology, engineering, and math (STEM) majors; Pizzolato, Chaudhari, Murrell, Podobnik, and Schaeffer (2008) employed ethnic identity and epistemological development theories to study academic achievement among students of color; and Jessup-Anger (2008) reviews research on identity development and gender identity to examine assumptions related to gender among a group of students participating in a 3-week study abroad program.

As another example, in Volume 31, Number 4 of *The Review of Higher Education,* Melguizo, Hagedorn, and Cypers (2008) apply human capital theory (Becker, 1964) and an equity framework (Levin, 2002) to assess the cost-effectiveness of community college attendance; Chang, Cerna, Han, and Sáenz (2008) employ anticipatory socialization theory and mismatch hypothesis to study the role of institutional status in retaining minorities in certain STEM majors; and Porter, Toutkoushian, and Moore (2008) allude to economic understandings that informed their analysis of unexplained wage gaps by gender and race in the academic

Table 7.1
Summary of theoretical frameworks presented in volume

Chapter	Theory	Student Sample	Discipline
1	Identity (Chickering, 1969)	n/a	Psychology
	Personality formation (Loevinger, 1976)		Psychology
	Moral development (Kohlberg, 1969)		Psychology
	Intellectual development (Perry, 1968)		Psychology
	Human capital (Bourdieu, 1977)		Sociology and Economics
	College impact theory (Terenzini et al., 1996)		Social psychology
	I-E-O theory (Astin, 1991)		Higher education
2	Retention (Tinto, 1993)	Black men at 4-year colleges	Sociology
3	College choice (Hossler & Gallagher, 1987)	First-year students at highly selective institutions	Social psychology
4	Challenge and support (Sanford, 1962)	African American males	Social psychology
5	College impact theory	First-generation collegians	Higher education
6	Sense of belonging (Hurtado & Carter, 1997; Tinto, 1993)	Latino collegians	Sociology
7	Ecological systems theory	n/a	Social psychology
	Technology adoption		Technology
	Critical race theory		Law
	Self-authorship		Psychology
	Resilience		Social psychology
	Socialization		Sociology

labor market. Most of these authors identify their theoretical framework explicitly; for instance, Chang et al. explain that anticipatory socialization refers to the process through which prospective members or novices (e.g., STEM undergraduates) begin to assume the values, attitudes, and practices of the group they wish to join (e.g., biomedical scientists). As an interesting counterpoint, other scholars have used anticipatory socialization theory to study working class students (Wegner, 1973); future faculty members (Tierney & Rhoads, 1993), and members of organizations (van Maanen, 1976).

Still, Volume 79, Number 1 of *The Journal of Higher Education* presents a few more examples in practice. Analyzing data from the Cooperative Institutional Research Program (CIRP) Freshman Survey, Bryant and Astin (2008) used spiritual struggle theory (Pargament, Murray-Swank, Magyar, & Ano, 2005) to identify the personal characteristics, orientations, and beliefs, for example, that predispose students to spiritual struggle; I used human and sociocultural capital theory to examine three labor market outcomes of African American college graduates (Strayhorn, 2008c); and Guillory and Wolverton (2008) adopt retention theory as a lens for studying Native American students in higher education. Readers are encouraged to look at published research studies to identify other theoretical frameworks like those mentioned above.

Consider reading qualitative research journals as well, including *The Qualitative Report*, *Anthropology and Education Quarterly*, and *The International Journal of Qualitative Studies in Education*, and *Qualitative Research*; this strategy may provide an impetus for creative applications in quantitative research on college students. I have used this approach recently to identify and understand alternate theories, which inform my most recent research. Although many of these studies have been presented at national and international conferences over the past year or so, most of the journal articles were "under review" or "in revision" at the time of this book's production. Therefore, they were not included as separate chapters in the volume. Instead, I provide a laconic overview of these theories in the next section.

Overview of Alternate Theories

By alternate, I simply mean "other" theories, beyond those reviewed in previous chapters, which can be applied in college student research. Alternate theories tend to cast new lights on social phenomena and thereby alter or change our understanding. Listed below are three summaries of such theories and a brief mention of how I have used them in the past year.

Critical Race Theory

Critical race theory (CRT) informs methods that challenge the ordinary nature of racism that characterizes contemporary society—racism of a more subtle sort, most times, than the conscious, violent expressions of pre-Civil Rights days (Bell, 1995). CRT critiques historical and structural conditions of oppression and seeks transformation of material conditions (Glesne, 2006). Most scholars agree that there are five tenets of CRT: (a) the centrality and intersectionality of race and racism, (b) the challenge to dominant ideology, (c) the commitment to social justice, (d) the importance of experiential knowledge, and (e) the use of an interdisciplinary perspective. In many ways, CRT draws attention to issues of power, oppression, privilege, representation, "voice," and responses to these forces.

CRT is considered a superior perspective for giving voice to minority cultural viewpoints. For instance, Bell (1995) employed CRT to explain why gross social disparities exist—and persist—in American society accompanied by deafening silence among Whites and economically disadvantaged individuals. His analysis suggests that the mass of Whites will accept huge inequities among Whites as long as White superiority over Blacks and other minorities is maintained. Based on analyses of this kind, I thought CRT would be useful in understanding the influence of state policies on race-based educational disparities (e.g., student achievement, college enrollment), the impact of culturally relevant pedagogy on Black and Latino student performance, and even the historical legacy of the first African American, Miss Alice Jackson, to apply for admission to my alma mater, The University of Virginia.

Ecological Systems Theory

Several recent works emphasize the "call to context" (Delgado, 1995, p. xv). To understand the relationship between individuals and significant or "instrumental others" (Ceja, 2006) in various contexts or systems (e.g., parents, teachers, siblings), it was necessary to find a theory that provided constructs for talking about the relationship between and within these structures. As Kerlinger (1986) explained, I defined theory as "a set of interrelated constructs, definitions, and propositions that presents a systematic view of phenomena by specifying relations among variables, with the purpose of explaining and predicting phenomena" (p. 9). Thus, a blended theoretical framework drawing on Bronfenbrenner's (1979) ecological systems theory and notions of cultural capital as described by Bourdieu (1977a) was constructed. Since cultural capital has been referenced in earlier chapters, this discussion will be limited to ecological systems theory only.

Bronfenbrenner's (1979) ecological systems theory describes four types of nested systems: microsystem, mesosystem, exosystem, and macrosystem. Each system contains roles, norms, and rules that shape one's development. Taken together, the four systems represent the nested networks of interactions that reflect an individual's ecology. This ecology changes over time as an individual gets older or as certain systems (e.g., peers, families, schools) become more or less salient to the individual's development; this refers to the chronosystem, which is often described as the fifth system.

Ecological systems theory has been useful to me in recent studies as it alludes to the ways in which parental involvement, achievement in school, and personal characteristics may converge and impact one's development. That is, the model holds significant assumptions about the ways in which school-level variables, family-level factors, and students' background traits interact and influence individual-level outcomes such as psychosocial development, behavior, academic achievement, and decisions to enroll in college. I have used the theory to study the college enrollment decisions of African American males at 4-year colleges, the influence of parental involvement on Black collegians academic achievement, and the impact of neighborhood effects on the educational aspirations of Black youth.

Resilience Theory

Research has consistently shown that resilience acts as an important buffer for students, especially those placed at-risk in educational settings. Resilience is defined in several ways; for instance, resilience is achievement when achievement is rare for those facing similar circumstances (Gayles, 2005). Wang and Gordon (1994) posited resilience as "success in schools despite personal vulnerabilities, adversities brought about by early and ongoing environmental conditions and experiences" (p. 38). Theoretically speaking, resilient youth should have high self-esteem, confidence in one's ability, and more positive educational outcomes than their peers who lack resilient qualities.

Drawing upon notions from resilience theory, I have conducted several survey studies to (a) identify barriers faced by economically disadvantaged students of color in the pathway to and through college (b) explain the role that resilience plays in their academic success and (c) recommend strategies for nurturing students' resilience. As described in earlier chapters, theory helped me build the argument for these studies, narrow each study's focus, create survey items that tap one's resiliency, and interpret findings. Similar to Connor-Davidson (2003), I asked students to rate the degree to which statements were reflective of them. A sample of the resilience scale includes, "When I run into setbacks, I am able to 'bounce back" readily." To date, I have found empirical support for the association between resilience and self-efficacy, self-esteem, and students' expectations about college.

Self-Authorship

Self-authorship is a theoretical lens, which allows researchers to examine and understand the meaning making processes that individuals employ to make a series of judgments, decisions, and interpretations about their experiences (e.g., Baxter Magolda, 2004). Self-authorship, as a constructive developmental theory, refers to "the ability to collect, interpret, and analyze information and reflect on one's own beliefs to form judgments" (Baxter Magolda, 1998, p. 143). Scholars tend to agree that self-authorship consists of three dimensions: cognitive, intrapersonal, and interpersonal. These three dimensions also suggest the major stages toward self-authorship: *The Crossroads, Becoming the Author of One's Life,* and *Internal Foundations* (Baxter Magolda, 2001).

As a doctoral student, I became familiar with self-authorship as a theoretical construct. I was first introduced to self-authorship through the work of Marcia Baxter Magolda, which was published in the *Journal of College Student Development* (JCSD). JCSD was one of several journals that I read religiously during my doctoral studies. When new issues arrived, I read them cover-to-cover. And, without intention, I always seemed to wrestle with articles on self-authorship. I wanted to know it as a distinct concept, to understand its key elements and assumptions, to think deeply about its relevance to college student research. Like most doctoral students at the point of dissertation, I had to suspend my curiosity for the moment to focus on the "book." I promised myself that I would "get in the ring" with self-authorship once I completed my degree, to understand its intricacies, its relevance to my own work.

Several years later as a tenure-track faculty member, I did just that. I had the opportunity to talk with several scholars who study self-authorship, including my major advisor's wife who uses the theory to study women's career choice (Creamer & Laughlin, 2005). Apart from indicating my general interest in the concept, I shared my desire to develop an instrument that assessed self-authorship as defined in the existing research. Those gathered encouraged me to pursue this line of work and I did so. To date, I have conducted survey studies to examine self-authorship and its influence on academic achievement among African Americans at historically Black colleges and economically disadvantaged Black students attending predominantly White institutions.

Socialization Theory

Scholars have emphasized the importance of socialization as the process by which individuals acquire what is needed to participate effectively in organizational life (Brim, 1966; Dunn, Rouse, & Seff, 1994). Generally speaking, socialization results in knowledge acquisition, which increases the probability of effective role performance. Socialization is defined by two core elements—investment and involvement—that lead to identification with and commitment to a professional role (Blackhurst, Brandt, & Kalinowski, 1998; Stein, 1992; Thornton & Nardi, 1975). Socialization can occur through undergraduate research programs, formal and informal faculty-student mentoring experiences, student organization meetings, graduate preparation programs, professional development workshops, and interactions with others.

Socialization theory has influenced my work on African American male graduate students, faculty-student mentoring, Black Greek-letter organizations, new professionals in student affairs, and historically underrepresented minorities in formal research-focused mentoring programs like the Ronald E. McNair Post-baccalaureate Scholars Program. More recent work focuses on gender socialization among African American gay male undergraduates at predominantly White institutions and the pre-tenure experiences of recently tenured Black faculty at research institutions.

Technology Adoption Model

Prior research highlights the relationship between features of various technologies and adoption or use of such technology (Rogers, 1986) in learning environments. Much of the theoretical work in this area emanates from Rogers' theory of technology diffusion. He identified five attributes by which technology innovations are judged: (a) trialability, (b) observability, (c) relative advantage, (d) complexity, and (e) compatibility. Thus, innovations that can be tried or tested, yield results that can be observed, and have an advantage over current processes are more likely to be adopted and distributed for broader use.

Related to Rogers' (1995) theory of technology diffusion, Davis (1989) posited a technology acceptance model (TAM) based on Fishbein and Azjen's (1975) reasoned action theory. TAM suggests that usage is a function of intention to use, while intention is determined by perceived usefulness and perceived ease of use. Perceived usefulness refers to "the degree to which a person believes that using a particular system would enhance his or her job performance" (Davis, p. 320). On the other hand, perceived ease of use refers to "the degree to which a person believes that using a particular system would be free of effort" (Davis, p. 320).

Recently, I have used TAM to study undergraduate students' use of Facebook, MySpace, and even online learning technologies such as Blackboard. Future work will protract this line of inquiry into areas such as technology's influence on academic achievement, college satisfaction, and sense of belonging.

New Directions for Future Research

The complexion of higher education in America has changed dramatically as a result of demographic shifts and social progress over the past 20 years (U.S. Department of Education, 2006). Consequently, "our baseline of knowledge is no longer adequate for the rapidly changing world that we live in" (Stage, 2007b, p. 97). This provides a stimulus for taking research in new directions and for imagining creative ways to incorporate theory in future research.

Indeed, much can be done. Both higher education scholars who specialize in interdisciplinary approaches and scholars from disciplines that span the social sciences and humanities might employ theories to explore a range of possible topics. Sociologists could investigate preparation of future faculty using socialization theory or how online social networks (e.g., Facebook) help or hinder campus community using social network-ing theory. Social psychologists could examine phenomena such as inter-actions, exchanges, and social movements using social identity theory, cross-racial interactionism, and perspectives on social inequality. Histo-rians could explore the evolution of campus units or "safe spaces" (e.g., Black cultural centers) using institutionalization theory. Economists could address the potential economic responses to state-supported merit aid scholarships, their effectiveness, and their costs and benefits using policy adoption models. Psychologists might consider how students as-sume values and beliefs different from their own using theories of intel-lectual and moral development, for instance. Political scientists might examine the ability of top-down vs. bottom up educational institutions to accommodate change brought about through student activism using ap-propriate theoretical perspectives. In most cases, researchers will want to cross multiple disciplinary boundaries, drawing from many areas of so-cial science and the humanities to answer key research questions.

A substantial literature has documented a wage gap between White and racially diverse college graduates. Almost all studies indicate race, gender, and academic major as significant drivers of such inequalities. What may differ across fields is the primary source of inequities. For instance, some graduates may earn less due to differences in roles, goals, and central tasks of one's position; on the other hand, graduates may face serious oppressions such as race or gender discrimination, marginaliza-tion of one's work, or even racism. Thus, future research might examine the extent to these factors explain wage disparities using CRT. While some social science research suggests that context is important when de-termining outcomes, more research is needed to make this argument in the context of higher education. Thus, it is imperative for future research to address the issue of contexts, settings, or ecological systems. Finally, recent accountability trends bring attention to the impact of college on students, which, in turn, call for more research on student learning and development. I suggest that this issue could be examined through institu-tional theory or even political frames that accent the role of power, coali-tions, and resources. Despite this list of recommendations, many ques-tions remain and the possibilities for using *Theoretical Frameworks in College Student Research* are endless. I leave those important decisions to you, gentle reader.

References

Adelman, C. (1999). *Answers in the toolbox: Academic intensity, attendance patterns, and bachelor's degree attainment*. Washington, DC: U.S. Department of Education, Office of Educational Research and Improvement.

Adelman, C. (2002). The relationship between urbanicity and educational outcomes. In W. G. Tierney & L. S. Hagedorn (Eds.), *Increasing access to college: Extending possibilities for all students* (pp. 35-63). Albany: State University of New York Press.

Alexander, K. L., & Eckland, B. K. (1975). Basic attainment processes: A replication and extension. *Sociology of Education, 48,* 457-495.

Alwin, D., & Otto, L. (1977). High school context effects on aspirations. *Sociology of Education, 50,* 259-273.

Anderson, C. (1994). "Dear prospective student": An analysis of admissions material from four universities. *College and University, 70,* 27-38.

Anfara, V. A., & Mertz, N. T. (2006). *Theoretical frameworks in qualitative research*. Thousand Oaks: Sage.

Arbona, C., & Nora, A. (2007). The influence of academic and environmental factors on Hispanic college degree attainment. *The Review of Higher Education, 30*(3), 247-269.

Argyris, C., & Schon, D. A. (1974). *Theory in practice: Increasing professional effectiveness*. San Francisco: Jossey-Bass.

Arredondo, M., & Knight, S. (2005-2006). Estimating degree attainment rates of freshmen: A campus perspective. *Journal of College Student Retention: Research, Theory, and Practice, 7*(1-2), 91-116.

Astin, A. W. (1975). *Preventing students from dropping out*. San Francisco: Jossey-Bass.

Astin, A. W. (1984). Student involvement: A developmental theory for higher education. *Journal of College Student Personnel, 25,* 297-308.

Astin, A. W. (1991). *Assessment for excellence: The philosophy and practice of assessment and evaluation in higher education*. New York: McMillan.

Astin, A. W. (1993). *What matters in college: Four critical years revisited*. San Francisco: Jossey-Bass.

Atwater, M. M., & Alick, B. (1990). Cognitive development and problem solving of Afro-American students in chemistry. *Journal of Research in Science Teaching, 27,* 157-172.

Austin, A. A., & McDermott, K. A. (2003-2004). College persistence among single mothers after welfare reform: An exploratory study. *Journal of College Student Retention: Research, Theory, and Practice, 5*(2), 93-114.

Ausubel, D. P. (1963). *The psychology of meaningful verbal learning.* New York: Grune and Stratton.

Bailey, D. F., & Moore, J. L., III. (2004). Emotional isolation, depression, and suicide among African American men: Reasons for concern. In C. Rabin (Ed.), *Linking lives across borders: Gender-sensitive practice in international perspective* (pp. 186-207). Pacific Grove, CA: Brooks/Cole.

Baird, L. (1993). Using research and theoretical models of graduate student progress. In L. Baird (Ed.), *Increasing graduate student retention and degree attainment* (pp. 3-12). San Francisco: Jossey-Bass Publishers.

Baker, S., & Pomerantz, N. (2000-2001). Impact of learning communities on retention at a metropolitan university. *Journal of College Student Retention: Research, Theory, and Practice, 2*(2), 115-126.

Bank, B. J., Biddle, B. J., & Slavings, R. L. (1990). Effects of peer, faculty, and parental influences on student persistence. *The Sociological Quarterly, 63*, 208-225.

Baum, S., & Payea, K. (2004). *Education pays 2004.* New York: The College Board.

Baxter Magolda, M. B. (1998). Developing self-authorship in young adult life. *Journal of College Student Development, 39*, 143-156.

Baxter Magolda, M. B. (2004). Learning partnerships model: A framework for promoting self-authorship. In M. B. Baxter Magolda & P. M. King (Eds.), *Learning partnerships: Theory and models of practice to educate for self-authorship* (pp. 37-62). Sterling, VA: Stylus.

Baxter Magolda, M. B. (2008). Three elements of self-authorship. *Journal of College Student Development, 49*(4), 269-284.

Bean, J. P. (1980). Dropouts and turnover: The synthesis and test of a causal model of student attrition. *Research in Higher Education, 12*(2), 155-171.

Bean, J. P. (1982). Student attrition, intentions, and confidence: Interaction effects in a path model. *Research in Higher Education, 17*(4), 291-320.

Bean, J. P., & Metzner, B. S. (1985). A conceptual model of nontraditional undergraduate student attrition. *Review of Educational Research, 55*(4), 485-540.

Becker, G. S. (1964). *Human capital: A theoretical and empirical analysis with special reference to higher education.* New York: Columbia University Press.

Bell, D. (1995). Racial realism--After we've gone: Prudent speculations on America in a post-racial epoch. In R. Delgado (Ed.), *Critical race theory: The cutting edge* (pp. 2-8). Philadelphia: Temple University Press.

Bensimon, E. M. (2007). Presidential address: The underestimated significance of practitioner knowledge in the scholarship on student success. *The Review of Higher Education, 30*(4), 441-469.

Berry, I., R. Q. (2005). Voices of success: Descriptive portraits of two successful African American male middle school mathematics students. *Journal of African American Studies, 8*(4), 46-62.

Besnier, N. (1995). The appeal and pitfalls of cross-disciplinary dialogues. In J. A. Russell, J. M. Fernandez-Dols, A. S. R. Manstead & J. C. Wellenkamp (Eds.), *Everyday conceptions of emotion: An introduction to the psychology, anthropology, and linguistics of emotion* (pp. 559-570). Netherlands: Kluwer Academic Publishers.

Billson, J. M., & Terry, M. B. (1982). In search of the silken purse: Factors in attrition among first-generation students. *College and University, 58,* 57-75.

Blackhurst, A., Brandt, J., & Kalinowski, J. (1998). Effects of personal and work-related attributes on the organizational commitment and life satisfaction of women student affairs administrators. *NASPA Journal, 35*(2), 86-99.

Blau, P. M. (1964). *Exchange and power in social life.* New York: Wiley.

Bonner, F. A., II. (2001). *Gifted African American male college students: A phenomenological study.* Storrs, CT: National Research Center on the Gifted and Talented.

Bourdieu, P. (1977a). Cultural reproduction and social reproduction. In J. Karabel & A. Halsey (Eds.), *Power and ideology in education* (pp. 487-510). New York: Oxford University Press.

Bourdieu, P. (1977b). *Outline of a theory of practice.* Cambridge: Cambridge University Press.

Bowman, S. L., & York-Anderson, D. C. (1991). Assessing the knowledge of first-generation and second-generation college students. *Journal of College Student Development, 32*(2), 116-122.

Boyle, R. P. (1966). The effect of high school on student aspirations. *American Journal of Sociology, 71,* 628-639.

Braxton, J. M. (2000a). Introduction: Reworking the student departure puzzle. In J. M. Braxton (Ed.), *Reworking the student departure puzzle* (pp. 1-8). Nashville: Vanderbilt University Press.

Braxton, J. M. (2000b). Reinvigorating theory and research on the departure puzzle. In J. M. Braxton (Ed.), *Reworking the student departure puzzle* (pp. 257-274). Nashville: Vanderbilt University Press.

Braxton, J. M. (Ed.). (2000c). *Reworking the student departure puzzle.* Nashville: Vanderbilt University Press.

Brim, O. G. (1966). Socialization through the life cycle. In O. G. Brim & S. Wheeler (Eds.), *Socialization after childhood* (Vol. John Wiley and Sons, pp. 3-49). New York: NY.

Bronfenbrenner, U. (1979). *The ecology of human development.* Cambridge, MA: Harvard University Press.

Brown, L. L., & Robinson Kurpius, S. E. (1997). Psychosocial factors influencing academic persistence of American Indian college students. *Journal of College Student Development, 38,* 3-12.

Bryant, A. N., & Astin, H. S. (2008). The correlates of spiritual struggle during the college years. *The Journal of Higher Education, 79*(1), 1-27.

Canady, D. M. (2007). African American male college dropouts: Expectations of and experiences with an historically Black university's customer service delivery and student service provisions and implications for retention. *Dissertation Abstracts International, 68*(1A), 32.

Carnegie Foundation for the Advancement of Teaching. (2000). *A classification of institutions of higher education.* Princeton, NJ: Carnegie Council for the Advancement of Teaching.

Carter, D. F., & Hurtado, S. (2007). Bridging key research dilemmas: Quantitative research using a critical eye. In F. K. Stage (Ed.), *Using quantitative data to answer critical questions* (pp. 25-35). San Francisco: Jossey-Bass.

Carter, P. L. (2005). *Keepin' it real: School success beyond Black and White.* New York: Oxford University Press.

Castellanos, J., & Jones, L. (2003). Latina/o undergraduate experiences in American higher education. In J. Castellanos & L. Jones (Eds.), *The majority in the minority: Expanding the representation of Latina/o faculty, administrators, and students in higher education* (pp. 1-14). Sterling, VA: Stylus Publishing, LLC.

Ceja, M. (2006). Understanding the role of parents and siblings as information sources in the college choice process of Chicana students. *Journal of College Student Development, 47*(1), 87-104.

Chang, M. J. (2001). The positive educational effects of racial diversity on campus. In G. Orfield & M. Kurlaender (Eds.), *Diversity challenged: Evidence on the impact of affirmative action* (pp. 175-186). Cambridge, MA: The Civil Rights Project, Harvard Education Publishing Group.

Chang, M. J., Cerna, O., Han, J., & Sáenz, V. (2008). The contradictory roles of institutional status in retaining underrepresetned minorities in biomedical and behavioral science majors. *The Review of Higher Education, 31*(4), 433-464.

Chickering, A. W. (1969). *Education and identity.* San Francisco: Jossey-Bass.

Chickering, A. W. (2004). Adding value: Learning communities and student engagement. *Research in Higher Education, 45*(2), 115-138.

Chickering, A. W., & Reisser, L. (1993). *Education and identity* (2nd ed.). San Francisco: Jossey-Bass.

Choy, S. P. (2001). *Findings from the Condition of Education 2001: Students who parents did not go to college: Postsecondary access, persistence, and attainment* (NCES 2001-136). Washington, DC: U.S. Government Printing Office.

Cole, D., & Espinoza, A. (2008). Examining the academic success of Latino students in science technology engineering and mathematics (STEM) majors. *Journal of College Student Development, 49*(4), 285-300.

Coleman, J. S. (1988). Social capital in the creation of human capital. *American Journal of Sociology, 94 Supplement*, 95-120.

Connor, K. M., & Davidson, J. R. T. (2003). Development of a new resilience scale: The Connor-Davidson Resilience Scale (CD-RISC). *Depression and Anxiety, 18*(2), 76-82.

Creamer, D. G., & Associates. (1990). *College student development: Theory and practice for the 1990s.* Washington, DC: American College Personnel Association.

Creamer, E. G., & Laughlin, A. (2005). Self-authorship and women's career decision making. *Journal of College Student Development, 46*(1), 13-27.

Crotty, M. (1998). *The foundation of social research: Meaning and perspective in the research process.* Thousand Oaks, CA: Sage.

Cruce, T. M., Wolniak, G. C., Seifert, T. A., & Pascarella, E. T. (2006). Impacts of good practices on cognitive development, learning orientations, and graduate degree plans during the first year of college. *Journal of College Student Development, 47*(4), 365-383.

Cuyjet, M. J. (1997). African American men on college campuses: Their needs and their perceptions. In M. J. Cuyjet (Ed.), *Helping African American Men Succeed in College* (pp. 5-16). San Francisco: Jossey-Bass.

Cuyjet, M. J., & Associates (Eds.). (2006). *African American men in college.* San Francisco: Jossey-Bass.

Davis, F. D. (1989). Perceived usefulness, perceived ease of use, and user acceptance of information technology. *MIS Quarterly, 13*(3), 319-340.

Davis, J. E. (2001). Black boys at school: Negotiating masculinities and race. In R. Majors (Ed.), *Educating our Black children: New directions and radical approaches* (pp. 169-182). New York: RoutledgeFalmer.

Davis, J. E. (2003). Early schooling and academic achievement of African American males. *Urban Education, 38*(5), 515.

Delgado, R. (1995). Introduction. In R. Delgado (Ed.), *Critical race theory: The cutting edge* (pp. xiii-xvi). Philadelphia: Temple University Press.

Dixon, P. N., & Martin, N. K. (1991). Measuring factors that influence college choice. *NASPA Journal, 29*(1), 31-36.

Douglas, M. (1982). *In the active voice.* London: Routledge and Kegan Paul.

Dunn, D., Rouse, L., & Seff, M. A. (1994). New faculty socialization in the academic workplace. In J. C. Smart (Ed.), *Higher education: Theory and research* (Vol. 10, pp. 374-416). New York: Agathon.

Elliott, K. M., & Shin, D. (2002). Student satisfaction: An alternative approach to assessing this important concept. *Journal of Higher Education Policy and Management, 24,* 197-209.

Ellwood, D. T., & Kane, T. J. (2000). Who is getting a college education? Family background and the growing gaps in enrollment. In S. Danziger & J. Waldfogel (Eds.), *Securing the future: Investing in children from birth to college* (pp. 283-324). New York: Russell Sage Foundation.

Evans, N. J., Forney, D. S., & Guido-DiBrito, F. (1998). *Student development in college: Theory, research, and practice.* San Francisco: Jossey-Bass.

Ferguson, A. A. (2000). *Bad boys: Public schools in the making of Black male masculinity.* Ann Arbor: The University of Michigan Press.

Festinger, L. (1957). *A theory of cognitive dissonance.* Evanston, IL: Row, Peterson, & Company.

Fidler, P. P. (1991). Relationship of freshman orientation seminars to sophomore return rates. *Journal of the Freshman Year Experience, 3*(1), 7-38.

Fishbein, M., & Ajzen, I. (1975). *Belief, attitude, intention, and behavior: An introduction to theory and research.* Reading, MA: Addison-Wesley.

Fleming, J. (1981). Special needs of Blacks and other minorities. In A. W. Chickering & Associates (Eds.), *The modern American college: Responding to the new realities of diverse students and a changing society.* San Francisco: Jossey-Bass.

Flowers, L. A. (2003). Effects of college racial composition on African American students' interactions with faculty. *College Student Affairs Journal, 23,* 54-63.

Freeman, K. (1997). Increasing African Americans' participation in higher education: African American high school students' perspective. *Journal of Higher Education, 68*(5), 523-550.

Freeman, K. (1999). The race factor in African Americans' college choice. *Urban Education, 34,* 4-25.

Freeman, K. (2005). *African Americans and college choice: The influence of family and school.* Albany: State University of New York Press.

Freeman, T. M., Anderman, L. H., & Jensen, J. M. (2007). Sense of belonging in college freshmen at the classroom and campus levels. *The Journal of Experimental Education, 75*(3), 203-220.

Fries-Britt, S. L. (1997). Identifying and supporting gifted African American men. In M. J. Cuyjet (Ed.), *Helping African American men succeed in college* (pp. 65-78). San Francisco: Jossey-Bass.

Furstenberg, F. F., & Hughes, M. E. (1995). Social capital and successful development among at-risk youth. *Journal of Marriage and the Family, 57,* 580-592.

Gándara, P. (1995). *Over the ivy walls: The educational mobility of low-income Chicanos.* Albany: State University of New York Press.

Gándara, P. (2002). Meeting common goals: Linking K-12 and college interventions. In W. G. Tierney & L. S. Hagedorn (Eds.), *Increasing access to college: Extending possibilities for all students* (pp. 81-103). Albany: State University of New York Press.

Gayles, J. (2005). Playing the game and paying the price: Academic resilience among three high-achieving African American males. *Anthropology & Education Quarterly, 36*(3), 250-264.

Geertz, C. (1973). Thick description: Toward an interpretive theory of culture. In C. Geertz (Ed.), *The interpretation of cultures* (pp. 3-30). New York: Basic Books.

Gibbs, J. T. (Ed.). (1988). *Young, black, and male in America: An endangered species*. Dover, MA: Auburn House.

Gilmore, J. E., Spiro, L. M., & Dolich, I. J. (1981). How high school students select a college. University Park, PA: Pennsylvania State University.

Glesne, C. (2006). *Becoming qualitative researchers: An introduction* (3rd ed.). Boston, MA: Pearson Education, Inc.

Gonyea, R. M., Kish, K. A., Kuh, G. D., Muthiah, R. N., & Thomas, A. D. (2003). *College Student Experiences Questionnaire: Norms for the Fourth Edition*. Bloomington, IN: Indiana University Center for Post-secondary Research, Policy, and Planning.

Goodenow, C. (1993). The psychological sense of school membership among adolescents: Scale development and educational correlates. *Psychology in the Schools, 30*, 79-90.

Guiffrida, D. A. (2004). Friends from home: Asset and liability to African American students attending a predominantly White institution. *NASPA Journal, 24*, 693-708.

Guiffrida, D. A. (2005). To break away or strengthen ties to home: A complex question for African American students attending a predominantly White institution. *Equity & Excellence in Education, 38*(1), 49-60.

Guillory, R. M., & Wolverton, M. (2008). It's about family: Native American student persistence in higher education. *The Journal of Higher Education, 79*(1), 58-87.

Hagedorn, L. S., & Tierney, W. G. (2002). Cultural capital and the struggle for educational equity. In W. G. Tierney & L. S. Hagedorn (Eds.), *Increasing access to college: Extending possibilities for all students* (pp. 1-11). Albany: State University of New York Press.

Hamilton, J. P. (2005). Reasons why African American men persist to degree completion in institutions of higher education. *Dissertation Abstracts International, A65*(10), 3717.

Harper, S. R. (2003). Most likely to succeed: The self-perceived impact of involvement on the experiences of high-achieving African American undergraduate men at predominantly White universities. *Dissertation Abstracts International, A64*(6), 1995.

Harris, E. L. (2006). Mary Douglas's typology of grid and group. In V. A. Anfara, Jr. & N. T. Mertz (Eds.), *Theoretical frameworks in qualitative research* (pp. 129-154). Thousand Oaks, CA: Sage.

Hatcher, L., Kryter, K., Prus, J. S., & Fitzgerald, V. (1992). Predicting college student satisfaction, commitment, and attrition from investment model constructs. *Journal of Applied Social Psychology, 22,* 1273-1296.

Hausmann, L. R. M., Schofield, J. W., & Woods, R. L. (2007). Sense of belonging as a predictor of intentions to persist among African American and White first-year college students. *Research in Higher Education, 48*(7), 803-839.

Hearn, J. C. (1984). The relative roles of academic, ascribed, and socioeconomic characteristics in college destinations. *Sociology of Education, 57,* 22-30.

Hearn, J. C. (1987). Impacts of undergraduate experiences on aspirations and plans for graduate and professional education. *Research in Higher Education, 27,* 119-141.

Hearn, J. C. (1990). Pathways to attendance at the elite colleges. In P. W. Kingston & L. S. Lewis (Eds.), *The high-status track: Studies of elite schools and stratification* (pp. 121-145). New York: SUNY Press.

Hearn, J. C. (1991). Academic and nonacademic influences on the college destinations of 1980 high school graduates. *Sociology of Education, 64*(3), 158-171.

Heath, S. B., & McLaughlin, M. W. (1987). A child resource policy: Moving beyond dependence on school and family. *Phi Delta Kappan, 68,* 576-580.

Henstrand, J. L. (2006). Seeking an understanding of school culture: Using theory as a framework for observation and analysis. In V. A. Anfara & N. T. Mertz (Eds.), *Theoretical frameworks in qualitative research* (pp. 1-22). Thousand Oaks: Sage.

Hochschild, J. L. (1995). *Facing up to the American dream: Race, class, and the soul of the nation.* Princeton: Princeton University Press.

Hoffman, M., Richmond, J., Morrow, J., & Salomone, K. (2002-2003). Investigating sense of belonging in first-year college students. *Journal of College Student Retention: Research, Theory, & Practice, 4*(3), 227-256.

Hossler, D. (1985). *A research overview of student college choice.* Paper presented at the annual meeting of the Association for the Study of Higher Education, Chicago, IL.

Hossler, D., Braxton, J. M., & Coopersmith, G. (1989). Understanding student college choice. In J. C. Smart (Ed.), *Higher education: Handbook of theory and research* (Vol. 5, pp. 231-288). New York: Agathon Press.

Hossler, D., & Gallagher, K. S. (1987). Studying student college choice: A three-phase mdoel and the implications for policymakers. *College and University, 62,* 207-221.

Hossler, D., Schmit, J. L., & Vesper, N. (1999). *Going to college: how social, economic, and educational factors influence the decisions students make.* Baltimore: Johns Hopkins University Press.

Hrabowski, F. A., III, Maton, K. I., & Greif, G. L. (1998). *Beating the odds: Raising academically successful African American males.* New York: Oxford University Press.

Hurtado, S., & Carter, D. F. (1997). Effects of college transition and perceptions of campus racial climate on Latino college students' sense of belonging. *Sociology of Education, 70*(4), 324-345.

Inman, E. W., & Mayes, L. (1999). The importance of being first: Unique characteristics of first-generation community college students. *Community College Review, 26*(4), 3-23.

Ishitani, T. T. (2003). A longitudinal approach to assessing attrition behavior among first-generation students: Time-varying effects of pre-college characteristics. *Research in Higher Education, 44*(4), 433-449.

Jackson, G. (1982). Public efficiency and private choice in higher education. *Educational Evaluation and Policy Analysis, 4*, 237-247.

Jackson, J. F. L. (2003). Toward administrative diversity: An analysis of the African-American male educational pipeline. *The Journal of Men's Studies, 12*, 43-60.

Jackson, R., & Chapman, R. (1984). *The influence of no-need aid and other factors on college choices of high ability students.* Paper presented at the The College Board Annual Forum, New York.

Jackson, R. L., III, & Crawley, R. L. (2003). White student confessions about a Black male professor: A cultural contracts theory approach to intimate conversations about race and worldview. *The Journal of Men's Studies, 12*, 25-41.

Jakobson, R. (1987). On realism in art. In K. Pomorska & S. Rudy (Eds.), *Language in literature* (pp. 25-26). Cambridge, MA: Harvard University Press.

Jessup-Anger, J. E. (2008). Gender observations and study abroad: How students reconcile cross-cultural differences related to gender. *Journal of College Student Development, 49*(4), 360-373.

Johnson, D. R., Soldner, M., Leonard, J. B., Alvarez, P., Inkelas, K. K., Rowan-Kenyon, H., et al. (2007). Examining sense of belonging among first-year undergraduates from different racial/ethnic groups. *Journal of College Student Development, 48*(5), 525-542.

Jones, S. R. (1997). Voices of identity and difference: A qualitative exploration of the multiple dimensions of identity development in women college students. *Journal of College Student Development, 38*(4), 376-385.

Jones, S. R., & McEwen, M. K. (2000). A conceptual model of multiple dimensions of identity. *Journal of College Student Development, 41*(4), 405-414.

Justiz, M. J., & Rendon, L. I. (1989). Hispanic students. In M. L. Upcraft, J. N. Gardner & Associates (Eds.), *The freshman year experience: Helping students survive and succeed in college* (pp. 261-276). San Francisco: Jossey-Bass.

Karabel, J., & Astin, A. W. (1975). Social class, academic ability, and college quality. *Social Forces, 53*, 381-398.

Kearney, K. S., & Hyle, A. E. (2006). A look through the Kubler-Ross theoretical lens. In V. A. Anfara, Jr. & N. T. Mertz (Eds.), *Theoretical frameworks in qualitative research* (pp. 109-128). Thousand Oaks, California: Sage.

Kegan, R. (1994). *In over our heads: The mental demands of modern life*. Cambridge, MA: Harvard Press.

Keith, T. Z. (2006). *Multiple regression and beyond*. Boston, MA: Pearson.

Kerlinger, F. N. (1986). *Foundations of behavioral research* (3rd ed.). New York: Holt, Rinehart, & Winston.

Kim, D. H., & Schneider, B. (2005). Social capital in action: Alignment of parental support in adolescents' transition to postsecondary education. *Social Forces, 84*(2), 1181-1206.

Kohlberg, L. (1969). Stage and sequence: The cognitive developmental approach to socialization. In D. A. Goslin (Ed.), *Handbook of socialization theory and research* (pp. 347-480). Chicago: Rand McNally.

Kotler, P. (1976). Applying marketing theory to college admissions. In College Entrance Examination Board (Ed.), *A role for marketing in college admissions*. New York: College Entrance Examination Board.

Kotler, P., & Fox, K. (1985). *Strategic marketing for educational institutions*. Englewood Cliffs, NJ: Prentice-Hall.

Kristen, A. R., & Brent, L. B. (2005). Leadership Identity Development Among Lesbian, Gay, Bisexual, and Transgender Student Leaders. *The NASPA Journal, 42*(3).

Kunjufu, J. (1986). *Countering the conspiracy to destroy Black boys*. Chicago, IL: African American Images.

Lareau, A. (2003). *Unequal childhoods: Class, race, and family life*. Berkeley: University of California Press.

LeCompte, M. D., & Preissle, J. (1993). *Ethnography and qualitative design in educational research* (2nd ed.). San Diego: Academic Press.

Levin, H. M. (2002). A comprehensive framework for evaluating educational vouchers. *Educational Evaluation and Policy Analysis, 24*(3), 159-174.

Lewin, K. (1936). *Principles of topological psychology*. New York: McGraw-Hill.

Litten, L. H. (1982). Different strokes in the applicant pool: Some refinements in a model of student choice. *Journal of Higher Education, 53*(4), 383-402.

Loevinger, J. (1976). *Ego development: Conceptions and theories*. San Francisco: Jossey-Bass.

Loevinger, J. (1998). History of the Sentence Completion Test (SCT) for ego development. In J. Loevinger (Ed.), *Technical foundations for measuring ego development: The Washington University Sentence Completion Test*. Mahwah, NJ: Lawrence Erlbaum Associates.

Loevinger, J., & Wessler, R. (1970). *Measuring ego development: Construction and use of a sentence completion test* (Vol. 1). San Francisco: Jossey-Bass.

London, H. B. (1989). Breaking away: A study of first-generation college students and their families. *American Journal of Education, 97,* 144-170.

Lucas, C. (1994). *American higher education: A history.* New York: St. Martin's Griffin.

MacLeod, J. (1995). *Ain't no makin' it: Aspirations and attainment in a low-income neighborhood.* Boulder, CO: Westview Press.

Majors, R., & Billson, J. (1992). *Cool pose: The dilemmas of Black manhood in America.* New York: Touchstone.

Malgwi, C. A., Howe, M. A., & Burnaby, P. A. (2005). Influences on Students' Choice of College Major. *Journal of Education for Business, 80*(5), 275-282.

Martin, W. E., Swartz-Kulstad, J. L., & Madson, M. (1999). Psychosocial factors that predict the college adjustment of first-year undergraduate students: Implications for college counselors. *Journal of College Counseling, 2,* 121-133.

Massey, D. S., Charles, C. Z., Lundy, G. F., & Fischer, M. J. (2003). *The source of the river: The social origins of freshmen at America's selective colleges and universities.* Princeton, NJ: Princeton University Press.

McCarron, G. P., & Inkelas, K. K. (2006). The gap between educational aspirations and attainment for first-generation college students and the role of parental involvement. *Journal of College Student Development, 47*(5), 534-549.

McDonough, P. M. (1997). *Choosing colleges: How social class and schools structure opportunity.* Albany, NY: State University of New York Press.

McDonough, P. M., antonio, A. L., & Trent, J. W. (1997). Black students, Black colleges: An African American college choice model. *Journal for a Just and Caring Education, 3,* 9-36.

Melguizo, T., Hagedorn, L. S., & Cypers, S. (2008). Remedial/ developmental education and the cose of community college transfer: A Los Angeles county sample. *The Review of Higher Education, 31*(4), 401-431.

Merriam, S. B. (1998). *Qualitative research and case study applications in education.* San Francisco: Jossey-Bass.

Metzner, B. S., & Bean, J. P. (1987). The estimation of a conceptual model of nontraditional undergraduate student attrition. *Research in Higher Education, 27*(1), 15-38.

Moore, J. L., III. (2000). Counseling African American men back to health. In L. Jones (Ed.), *Brothers of the academy: Up and coming Black scholars earning our way in higher education* (pp. 248-261). Herndon, VA: Stylus.

Moore, J. L., III, Flowers, L. A., Guion, L. A., Zhang, Y., & Staten, D. L. (2004). Improving the experiences of non-persistent African American males in engineering programs: Implications for success. *National Association of Student Affairs Professionals Journal, 7*, 105-120.

Morgan, G. (1986). *Images of organizations*. Newbury Park, CA: Sage.

Mortenson Research Seminar on Public Policy Analysis of Opportunity for Postsecondary Education. (2001). College participation by gender, age 18 to 24, 1967 to 2000. *Postsecondary Education Opportunity, 109*, 1-16.

Munro, B. (1981). Dropouts from higher education: path analysis of a national sample. *American Educational Research Journal, 18*(2), 133-141.

Murphy, P. E. (1981). Consumer buying roles in college choic: Parents' and students' perceptions. *College and University, 57*, 150-160.

Nettles, M. T., & Perna, L. W. (1997). *The African American education data book: Higher and adult education*. Fairfax, VA: Frederick D. Patterson Research Institute.

Noguera, P. A. (2003). The trouble with Black boys: The role and influence of environmental and cultural factors on the academic performance of African American males. *Urban Education, 38*, 431-459.

Nora, A. (1987). Determinants of retention among Chicano students: A structural model. *Research in Higher Education, 26*(1), 31-59.

Nora, A., & Cabrera, A. F. (1993). The construct validity of institutional commitment: A confirmatory factor analysis. *Research in Higher Education, 34*(2), 243-262.

Nora, A., Rendón, L. I., & Cuadraz, G. (1999). Access, choice, and outcomes: A profile of Hispanic students in higher education. In A. Tashakkori & S. H. Ochoa (Eds.), *Education of Hispanics in the United States: Politics, policies, and outcomes* (Vol. 16, pp. Readings on Equal Education). New York: AMS Press.

Oakes, J., Rogers, J., Lipton, M., & Morrell, E. (2002). The social construction of college access: Confronting the technical, cultural, and political barriers to low-income students of color. In W. G. Tierney & L. S. Hagedorn (Eds.), *Increasing access to college: Extending possibilities for all students* (pp. 105-121). Albany: State University of New York Press.

Okun, M. A., & Finch, J. F. (1998). The Big Five personality dimensions and the process of institutional departure. *Contemporary Educational Psychology, 23*(3), 233-256.

Oliver, M. L., Rodriguez, C. J., & Mickelson, R. A. (1985). Brown and black in white: The social adjustment and academic performance of Chicano and Black students in a predominantly White university. *The Urban Review, 17*(1), 3-23.

Pargament, K. I., Murray-Swank, N., Magyar, G., & Ano, G. (2005). Spiritual struggle: A phenomenon of interest to pscyhology and religion. In W. R. Miller & H. Delaney (Eds.), *Judeo-Christian perspectives on psy-*

chology: Human nature, motivation, and change (pp. 245-268). Washington, DC: APA Press.

Parham, T. A., & McDavis, R. J. (1987). Black men, an endangered species: Who's really pulling the trigger. *Journal of Counseling and Development, 66,* 24-27.

Parker, C. A. (1977). On modeling reality. *Journal of College Student Personnel, 18*(5), 419-425.

Pascarella, E. T. (1985). College environmental influences on learning and cognitive development: A critical review and synthesis. In J. C. Smart (Ed.), *Higher education: Handbook of theory and research* (Vol. 1, pp. 1-61). New York: Agathon.

Pascarella, E. T., & Chapman, D. W. (1983). A multi-institutional, path analytic validation of Tinto's model of college withdrawal. *American Educational Research Journal, 20,* 87-102.

Pascarella, E. T., & Terenzini, P. T. (1983). Predicting voluntary freshman year persistence/withdrawal behavior in a residential university: A path analytic validation of Tinto's model. *Journal of Educational Psychology, 75,* 215-226.

Pascarella, E. T., & Terenzini, P. T. (1991). *How college affects students: Findings and insights from twenty years of research.* San Francisco: Jossey-Bass.

Pascarella, E. T., & Terenzini, P. T. (1998). Studying college students in the 21st century: Meeting new challenges. *Review of Higher Education, 21,* 151-165.

Pascarella, E. T., & Terenzini, P. T. (2005). *How college affects students: A third decade of research* (Vol. 2). San Francisco: Jossey-Bass.

Perna, L. W. (2000). Differences in the decision to enroll in college among African Americans, Hispanics, and Whites. *Journal of Higher Education, 71,* 117-141.

Perna, L. W., & Titus, M. A. (2005). The relationship between parental involvement as social capital and college enrollment: An examination of racial/group differences. *Journal of Higher Education, 76,* 486-518.

Perry, W. G. (1968). *Forms of intellectual and ethical development in the college years: A scheme.* New York: Holt, Rinehart & Winston.

Perry, W. G. (1981). Cognitive growth and ethical growth: The making of meaning. In A. W. Chickering (Ed.), *The modern American college* (pp. 76-116). San Francisco: Jossey-Bass.

Perry, W. G., Jr. (1978). Sharing in the cost of growth. In C. A. Parker (Ed.), *Encouraging development in college students* (pp. 267-273). Minneapolis: University of Minnesota Press.

Piaget, J. (1977). *The moral judgement of the child* (M. Gabain, Trans.). Hardmondsworth, England: Penguin.

Pizzolato, J. E., Chaudhari, P., Murrell, E. D., Podobnik, S., & Schaeffer, Z. (2008). Ethnic identity, epistemological development, and academic achievement in underrepresented students. *Journal of College Student Development, 49*(4), 301-318.

Polite, V. C., & Davis, J. E. (Eds.). (1999). *African American males in school and society*. New York: Teachers College Press.

Porter, S. R., Toutkoushian, R. K., & Moore, J. V., III. (2008). Pay inequities for recenlty hired faculty, 1988-2004. *The Review of Higher Education, 31*(4), 465-487.

Pratt, P. A., & Skaggs, C. T. (1989). First generation college students: Are they at greater risk of attrition than their peers? *Research in Rural Education, 6*(2), 31-34.

Ream, R. K. (2003). Counterfeit social capital and Mexican American underachievement. *Educational Evaluation and Policy Analysis, 25*(3), 237-262.

Rendón, L. I., Jalomo, R. E., & Nora, A. (2000). Theoretical consideration in the study of minority student retention in higher education. In J. M. Braxon (Ed.), *Reworking the student departure puzzle* (pp. 127-156). Nashville, TN: Vanderbilt University Press.

Renn, K. A. (2000). Patterns of situational identity among biracial and multiracial college students. *The Review of Higher Education, 23*(4), 399-420.

Renn, K. A. (2006). Identity and leadership development in lesbian, gay, bisexual, and transgender student organizations. *Concepts & Connections: A publication for leadership educators, 14*(1), 1-3.

Renn, K. A. (2007). LGBT student leaders and queer activists: Identities of lesbian, gay, bisexual, transgender, and queer-identified college student leaders and activists. *Journal of College Student Development, 48*(3), 311-330.

Roach, R. (2001). Where are the Black men on campus? *Black Issues in Higher Education, 18*(6), 18-24.

Rogers, C. R. (1961). *On becoming a person*. Boston: Houghton Mifflin.

Rogers, E. M. (1986). *Communication: The new media in society*. New York: The Free Press.

Rosenberg, M., & McCullough, B. C. (1981). Mattering: Inferred significance and mental health among adolescents. *Research in Community Mental Health, 2*, 163-182.

Sanchez, B., Reyes, O., & Singh, J. (2006). Makin' it in college: The value of significant individuals in the lives of Mexican American adolescents. *Journal of Hispanic Higher Education, 5*(1), 48-67.

Sanford, N. (1966). *Self and society: Social change and individual development*. New York: Atherton.

Sanford, N. (Ed.). (1962). *The American college: A psychological and social interpretation of higher learning*. New York: Wiley.

Sewell, W. (1971). Inequality of opportunity for higher education. *American Sociological Review, 36*, 793-809.

Sigelman, L., & Tuch, S. A. (1997). Metastereotypes: Blacks' perceptions of Whites' stereotypes of Blacks. *Public Opinion Quarterly, 61*(1), 87-101.

Spady, W. G. (1970). Dropouts from higher education: An interdisciplinary review and synthesis. *Interchange, 1*, 64-85.

Spies, R. (1978). *The effects of rising costs on college choice: A study of the application decisions of high ability students.* New York: The College Entrance Examination Board.

Stage, F. K. (2007a). Answering critical questions using quantitative data. In F. K. Stage (Ed.), *Using quantitative data to answer critical questions* (pp. 5-16). San Francisco: Jossey-Bass.

Stage, F. K. (2007b). Moving from probabilities to possibilities: Tasks for quantitative criticalists. In F. K. Stage (Ed.), *Using quantitative data to answer critical questions* (pp. 95-100). San Francisco: Jossey-Bass.

Steele, C. M. (1997). A threat in the air: How stereotypes shape intellectual identity and performance. *American Psychologist, 52*, 613-629.

Steele, C. M. (1999). A threat in the air: How stereotypes shape intellectual identity and performance. In E. Y. Lowe, Jr. (Ed.), *Promise and dilemma: Perspectives on racial diversity and higher education* (pp. 92-128). Princeton, NJ: Princeton University Press.

Stein, E. L. (1992). *Socialization at a protestant seminary.* Unpublished doctoral dissertation, University of Pittsburgh, Pittsburgh.

Stein, J. L. (2007). Peer educators and close friends as predictors of male college students' willingness to prevent rape. *Journal of College Student Development, 48*(1), 75-89.

Strage, A. (1999). Social and academic integration and college success: Similarities and differences as a function of ethnicity and family education background. *College Student Journal, 33*, 198-205.

Strauss, A. (1995). *Qualitative analysis for social scientists.* Cambridge, UK: Cambridge University Press.

Strayhorn, T. L. (2005). More than money matters: An integrated model of graduate student persistence. *Dissertation Abstracts International, A66*(2), 519.

Strayhorn, T. L. (2006a). College in the information age: Gains associated with students' use of technology. *Journal of Interactive Online Learning, 5*(2), 143-155.

Strayhorn, T. L. (2006b). Factors influencing the academic achievement of first-generation college students. *NASPA Journal, 43*(4), 82-111.

Strayhorn, T. L. (2006c). *Frameworks for assessing learning and development outcomes.* Washington, DC: Council for the Advancement of Standards in Higher Education (CAS).

Strayhorn, T. L. (2006d). Influence of gender, race, and socioeconomic status on college choice: A National Longitudinal Survey of Freshmen (NLSF) investigation. *NASAP Journal, 9*(1), 100-117.

Strayhorn, T. L. (2008a). Examining the relationship between collaborative learning and perceived intellectual development among African American males in college. *Journal of Excellence in College Teaching, 19*(2&3), 31-50.

Strayhorn, T. L. (2008b). How college students' engagement affects personal and social learning outcomes [Electronic Version]. *Journal of College & Character,* X. Retrieved November 27, 2008 from http://collegevalues.org/pdfs/Strayhorn.pdf.

Strayhorn, T. L. (2008c). Influences on labor market outcomes of African American college graduates: A national study. *The Journal of Higher Education, 79*(1), 29-57.

Strayhorn, T. L. (2008d). Sentido de pertenencia: A hierarchical analysis predicting sense of belonging among Latino college students. *Journal of Hispanic Higher Education, 7*(4), 301-320.

Strayhorn, T. L. (2008e). The role of supportive relationships in facilitating African American males' success in college. *NASPA Journal, 45*(1), 26-48.

Strayhorn, T. L., & Hirt, J. B. (2008). Social justice and student affairs work at minority serving institutions. In M. B. Gasman, B. Baez & C. S. V. Turner (Eds.), *Understanding minority-serving institutions* (pp. 203-216). Albany: State University of New York Press.

Swail, W. S., Cabrera, A. F., & Lee, C. (2004). *Latino youth and the pathway to college.* Washington, DC: Educational Policy Institute.

Taylor, J. R., Turner, R. J., Noymer, A., Beckett, M. K., & Elliott, M. N. (2001). A longitudinal study of the role and significance of mattering to others for depressive symptoms. *Journal of Health and Social Behavior, 42,* 310-325.

Terenzini, P. T., Cabrera, A. F., & Bernal, E. M. (2001). *Swimming against the tide: The poor in American higher education* (College Board Research Report No. 2001-1). New York: The College Board.

Terenzini, P. T., Springer, L., Yaeger, P. M., Pascarella, E. T., & Nora, A. (1996). First generation college students: Characteristics, experiences, and cognitive development. *Research in Higher Education, 37*(1), 1-22.

Thelin, J. R. (2004). *A history of American higher education.* Baltimore, MD: Johns Hopkins University Press.

Thomas, S. L. (2000). Ties that bind: A social network approach to understanding student integration and persistence. *Journal of Higher Education, 71,* 591-615.

Thomas, S. L., & Perna, L. W. (2004). The opportunity agenda: A reexamination of postsecondary reward and opportunity. In J. C. Smart (Ed.), *Higher education: Handbook of theory and research* (Vol. 19, pp. 43-84). Dordrecht, NL: Kluwer Academic Publishers.

Thornton, R., & Nardi, R. M. (1975). The dynamics of role acquisition. *American Journal of Sociology, 80,* 870-885.

Tierney, W. G., Corwin, Z. B., & Colyar, J. E. (Eds.). (2005). *Preparing for college: Nine elements of effective outreach*. Albany: State University of New York Press.

Tierney, W. G., & Hagedorn, L. S. (Eds.). (2002). *Increasing access to college: Extending possibilities for all students*. Albany: State University of New York Press.

Tierney, W. G., & Rhoads, R. A. (1993). Postmodernism and critical theory in higher education: Implications for research and practice. In J. C. Smart (Ed.), *Higher education: Handbook of theory and research* (pp. 308-343). New York: Agathon.

Tinto, V. (1975). Dropout from higher education: A theoretical synthesis of recent research. *Review of Educational Research, 45*(1), 89-125.

Tinto, V. (1987). *Leaving college: Rethinking the causes and cures of student attrition* (1st ed.). Chicago: University of Chicago Press.

Tinto, V. (1993). *Leaving college: Rethinking the causes and cures of student attrition* (2nd ed.). Chicago: University of Chicago Press.

Tinto, V. (1998). Colleges as communities: Taking research on student persistence seriously. *Review of Higher Education, 21*(2), 167-177.

U. S. Department of Education. (2000). *The condition of education*. Washington, DC: US Government Printing Office.

U.S. Department of Education, National Center for Education Statistics,. (2006). *The condition of education 2006* (NCES 2006-071). Washington, DC: U.S. Government Printing Office.

van Maanen, J. (1976). Breaking in: Socialization to work. In R. Dubin (Ed.), *Handbook of work, organization, and society* (pp. 67-130). Chicago: Rand-McNally College Publishing.

Velez, W. (1985). Finishing college: The effects of college type. *Sociology of Education, 58*(3), 191-200.

Villalpando, O., & Solorzano, D. G. (2005). The role of culture in college preparation programs: A review of the research literature. In W. G. Tierney, Z. B. Corwin & J. E. Colyar (Eds.), *Preparing for college: Nine elements of effective outreach* (pp. 13-28). Albany: State University of New York Press.

Villalpando, O., & Solórzano, D. G. (2005). The role of culture in college preparation programs: A review of the research literature. In W. G. Tierney, Z. B. Corwin & J. E. Colyar (Eds.), *Preparing for college: Nine elements of effective outreach* (pp. 13-28). Albany: State University of New York Press.

Vogt, W. P. (1999). *Dictionary of statistics and methodology: A non-technical guide for the social sciences*. Thousand Oaks: Sage.

Wang, M. C., & Gordon, E. W. (1994). *Educational resilience in inner-city America: Challenges and prospects*. Hillsdale, NJ: Lawrence Erlbaum Associates, Inc.

Warburton, E. C., Bugarin, R., & Nunez, A. M. (2001). *Bridging the gap: Academic preparation and postsecondary success of first-generation students* (NCES Report 2001-153). Washington, DC: U.S. Department of Education, National Center for Education Statistics.

Weathersby, R. P. (1981). Ego development. In A. W. Chickering & Associates (Eds.), *The modern American college: Responding to the new realities of diverse students and a changing society* (pp. 51-75). San Francisco: Jossey-Bass.

Wegner, E. L. (1973). The effects of upward mobility: A study of working-status college students. *Sociology of Education, 46*(3), 263-279.

Weidman, J. (1989). Undergraduate socialization: A conceptual approach. In J. C. Smart (Ed.), *Higher education: Handbook of theory and research* (Vol. 5). New York: Agathon.

Williamson, D. R., & Creamer, D. G. (1988). Student attrition in 2- and 4-year colleges: Application of a theoretical model. *Journal of College Student Development, 29*, 210-217.

Zemsky, R., & Oedel, P. (1983). *The structure of college choice.* New York: College Board.

About the Author

Dr. Terrell Lamont Strayhorn is associate professor of higher education in the School of Educational Policy and Leadership within the College of Education and Human Ecology at The Ohio State University, where he also serves as Senior Research Associate in the Kirwan Institute for the Study of Race & Ethnicity, Faculty Affiliate in the Todd A. Bell National Resource Center for African American Males, and holds joint appointments in the Department of Africana Studies, Sexuality Studies, and Engineering Education within the College of Arts & Sciences. He is Director/Founder of the Center for Higher Education Research & Policy (CHERP). He earned a PhD in higher education from Virginia Tech, a MEd in educational policy from the University of Virginia, and a BA in music and religious studies from the University of Virginia. In addition, he earned two certificates of advanced graduate studies in race and social policy and graduate teaching. Previously, he served as research associate for the Council of Graduate Schools in Washington, DC and The Helix Group, a public health consulting firm in suburban Maryland, as well as associate professor and Special Assistant to the Provost at the University of Tennessee.

His research centers on studying how college impacts students with a particular focus on the experiences of students of color and other historically underrepresented, misrepresented, or disadvantaged individuals. Considerable research attention has been directed toward the experiences of Black men in college and this is an area in which he has significant expertise. Using advanced statistical methods, modeling techniques, and, where appropriate, rigorous qualitative methods, Professor Strayhorn seeks to understand how facets of inequality accumulate over time and cascade into long-term disparities that, without intervention, tend to have a profound effect on one's life and livelihood. His work crosses multiple disciplinary boundaries and draws upon theoretical underpinnings from many areas in the social sciences, humanities, and even law. Past member of the American College Personnel Association's (ACPA) Commission for the Assessment of Student Development Directorate, a second segment of his research agenda focuses on assessing student learning and development outcomes. Author of *Frameworks for Assessing Learning and Development Outcomes* (2006), *The Evolving Challenges of Black College Students* (2010), *College Students' Sense of Belonging* (2012) and several other volumes, his empirical research has been published in highly-regarded, peer-reviewed journals including *The Journal of Higher Education, Journal of College Student Development, Review of Higher Education, NASAP Journal, Oracle: Research Journal of the Association of Fraternity Advisors, NASPA Journal, Journal of Hispanic Higher Education, Urban Education,* and *Journal of Online Interactive Learning* to name a few. He is a member of several editorial boards for refereed journals in the field of higher education and student affairs including the *Journal of College Student Development, NASPA Journal, College Student Affairs Journal, The Qualitative Report, National Association for Student Affairs Professionals' Journal, Journal of the Professoriate,* and *Journal of College Student Retention: Research, Theory, & Practice.* He serves as editor of *Spectrum: A Journal on Black Men* and Associate Editor of the *NASAP Journal.*

Grants from federal, state, and research organizations have supported his research. These include, but are not limited to, the National Science Foundation (NSF), U.S. Department of Education, National Association of Student Financial Aid Administrators, American College Personnel Association, National Association of Student Personnel Administrators, Tennessee Higher Education Commission, Southern Association of College Student Affairs, and the UT Office of Research.

Strayhorn is recipient of the 2006 ACPA Emerging Scholar Award, 2006 Outstanding Junior Scholar Award conferred by the Council on Ethnic Participation within the Association for the Study of Higher Education, 2007 Benjamin L. Perry Professional Service Award from NASAP, and 2008 ACPA Annuit Coeptis Emerging Professional Award. Professor Strayhorn received the coveted 2009 ASHE Early Career/Promising Scholar Award. In 2008, he received a prestigious NSF Faculty Early Career Development (CAREER) award to support a 5-year project on identifying strategies that broaden participation of minorities, namely African American and Latino males, in science, technology, engineering, and math fields. In 2011, *Diverse Issues in Higher Education* named him one of the top 12 "Emerging Scholars" in the country.

Strayhorn is the proud father of two children, Aliyah Brielle Strayhorn and Tionne Lamont Strayhorn. He is a skilled pianist, loves to watch *CSI: Miami*, is a member of Alpha Phi Alpha Fraternity, Incorporated, and resides in Columbus, Ohio with Teddy, his Yorkshire terrier (smile).

Index